COLLECTING

Yellow Ware

An Identification and Value Guide

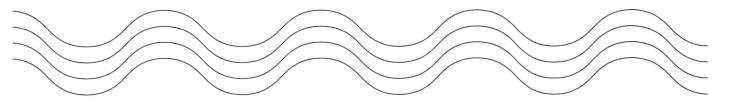

COLLECTING

Yellow Ware

An Identification and Value Guide

by
Lisa S. McAllister   John L. Michel

COLLECTOR BOOKS
A Division of Schroeder Publishing Co., Inc.

The current values in this book should be used only as a guide. They are not intended to set prices, which vary from one section of the country to another. Auction prices as well as dealer prices vary greatly and are affected by condition as well as demand. Neither the Authors nor the Publisher assumes responsibility for any losses that might be incurred as a result of consulting this guide.

Searching For A Publisher?

We are always looking for knowledgeable people considered to be experts within their fields. If you feel that there is a real need for a book on your collectible subject and have a large comprehensive collection, contact us.

COLLECTOR BOOKS
P.O. Box 3009
Paducah, Kentucky 42002-3009

Additional copies of this book may be ordered from:

COLLECTOR BOOKS
P.O. Box 3009
Paducah, Kentucky 42002-3009

@$16.95. Add $2.00 for postage and handling.

Copyright: Lisa S. McAllister, John L. Michel, 1993

1 2 3 4 5 6 7 8 9 0

Printed by IMAGE GRAPHICS, INC., Paducah, Kentucky

DEDICATION

To Barbara Michel who constantly provided encouragement and insight and never questioned the weekends lost to antique shows, museums, and libraries.

–John L. Michel

To yellow ware collectors for whom we have provided more pieces of the yellow ware puzzle.

–Lisa S. McAllister

ACKNOWLEDGMENTS

Photography By:
Sara Dillow
Lisa McAllister
John Michel
Roy David Farris
Wendell Abernathy
Ivan Clifford
Howard Foster

**Very special thanks
from Lisa McAllister to:**
Sara Dillow, without whom this book could not have been made

Barry McAllister, who became the "woman what does" so that I could finish this book

Anne Schwiebert and the late Lou Schwiebert for expanding my horizons, literally and figuratively

Special mention to:
Bill Putzier, for taking the time to send important information

Firstlook Photo-Longmeadow Branch, Hagerstown, MD

Lisa Stroup, who provided encouragement and guidance

Items from the collection of:
Byron and Sara Dillow
Wendell Abernathy
Howie and Iris Hirsch
Alicia Lampe
John and Barbara Michel
Lisa McAllister
Kate Wittenberg
Ivan and Gladys Clifford
Glenna Fitzgerald
Bernice Woolsey
Howard Foster
Murray Weinberg

TABLE OF CONTENTS

INTRODUCTION

England began to export quantities of yellow ware to the United States in the early 1800's. However, it was not long before "Yankee ingenuity" aided by the migration of British potters to our shores meant that the ware was being domestically produced in quantity. The abundance of clay, good transportation systems and large population centers made the East Coast an ideal location. Various sized potteries sprang up in states such as New Jersey, New York, Vermont, and Pennsylvania. Due to the efforts of David Henderson, New Jersey soon became the creative leader in the production of yellow ware. However, as the nation moved west, so did the production of yellow ware. Ohio soon became the leader in both the number of potteries and pieces produced. Although yellow ware manufacturers were able to withstand intense domestic competition, recessions, a civil war, strikes, and British imports, they fell victim to changing tastes. By the end of the 19th century, whitewares were becoming the choice of most households. Potters either stopped producing yellow ware or produced both wares. If the latter was the case, yellow ware production was limited. Although yellow ware lost its momentum, production continued well into the 20th century.

Yellow ware has established its place in America's ceramic continuum. It proved to be superior to redware and became the workhorse of the kitchen. This role has caused it to be called utilitarian. It unknowingly bridged the gap between redware and whiteware. Thus, it has been called transitional. Regardless of how one wants to define the ware, it is an integral and collectable part of our past.

To facilitate the presentation of material, this book is divided into three parts. Part I discusses how yellow ware was formed, decorated, and fired. The more technical aspects have been omitted so that the presentation will not get bogged down in excessive detail. Part II selectively discusses the potters and potteries that produced yellow ware. The vast majority of manufacturers neither marked their wares nor made any significant contribution to the state of the art. Because it is not the intent of this work to present a laundry list of names, dates, and locations, this type of manufacturer has been omitted. The reader should bear in mind that even those manufacturers who marked their wares often produced the same pieces in the same manner as every other pottery. At the end of Part II is a list of manufacturers who marked their ware. Part III is the identification guide. The intention of this section is to provide a representative sample of each form. Because it is impossible to illustrate and price every possible variation, it is hoped that the reader can estimate a fair market value for pieces not pictured by using similar pieces as a guide. The bibliography lists works that the reader can consult to broaden his or her knowledge of the field.

Part I

THE MANUFACTURING PROCESS

Redware

Prior to the introduction of yellow ware, redware was the earthenware in common use. Made from lower glacial clay, it was fired at 1800°F for 36 hours to produce a finished piece. Depending on the amount of iron in the clay, the color actually ranged from light tan to deep reddish brown. Because redware was fragile, porous, and covered with a lead-based glaze, it was impractical for everyday use. Applied to the piece before firing, the clear glaze was a mixture of silica, lead, and kaolin. Because silica melts at a high temperature, lead had to be added as a glaze flux to lower the temperature at which the glaze would fuse with the piece. Colored glazes were made by adding various oxides to the clear glaze mixture. Depending on the amount added, iron oxide produced a light yellow to dark brown color, copper oxide produced a green color, and manganese produced a dark brown to black color.

Stoneware

Stoneware was also commonly used, especially for storage. Although heavier than redware, it had the advantage of being non-porous. The clay used in its production was fired at 2300°F for up to five days. Given the drab appearance of the ware, a salt glaze was applied to enhance its appearance. During the firing, salt was thrown into the kiln. Heat converted the salt to sodium oxide which interacted with the silica in the clay to form a glaze on the piece. To further enhance the aesthetics, designs were painted in cobalt blue and sometimes brown. These designs range from very simple to complex. Certain pieces also had a brown glaze called Albany slip applied to the interior surface. This was done because the salt glaze only covered the exterior of the piece. Albany slip was also applied to the entire body, except the base, of some pieces.

Yellow ware

Made from finer clay, yellow ware was sturdier than redware and less dense than stoneware. Because the clay had to be fired to 2200°F to produce a hardened piece, a second firing, sometimes called a gloss firing, was necessary to apply the glaze. The first firing, also known as the biscuit firing, produced a mature piece which was porous. At first, a lead-based glaze which was similar to the one used on redware was applied. However, an alkaline-based glaze consisting of flint, kaolin, and white lead quickly came into use.

The Clay

Although the size of potteries varied greatly, the preparation of the clay followed the same general procedure. The first step in the process was to obtain the clay. Larger potteries and those far from natural deposits were likely to purchase the clay from suppliers. Smaller potteries, especially one and two person operations, usually obtained the clay from local deposits in stream beds and hillsides. Once the clay was obtained and large impurities were removed, it had to be aged in a cool place. This aging process took from six to 12 months. When the aging process was completed, the clay had to be refined to a workable consistency. Smaller potteries used a device similar to a butter churn to accomplish this task. Larger operations used a pug mill. A pug mill was a vat with a central revolving post to which blades were attached below the rim of the vat. Horizontal bars were attached to a post at a height above the rim of the vat so that a horse or two men could use them to turn the post. Once the clay was brought to its proper consistency, it was rolled into balls appropriate in weight for the pieces to be made and stored in a cool place. When the potter was ready to work, a ball of clay was taken from storage, dampened, and kneaded to remove any air bubbles.

Forming The Piece

During the infancy of yellow ware production, most pieces were turned or thrown on a potter's wheel. After the clay had been properly prepared, it was centered on the wheel. Then, as the wheel turned, the potter would form the piece by using his thumbs to determine the thickness and his fingers to shape the piece. Throughout this process, the clay had to be kept wet. In addition to using his hands, the potter used implements known as ribs to form and shape the piece. When the forming was complete, the piece was separated from the wheel by drawing a wire between its base and the wheel.

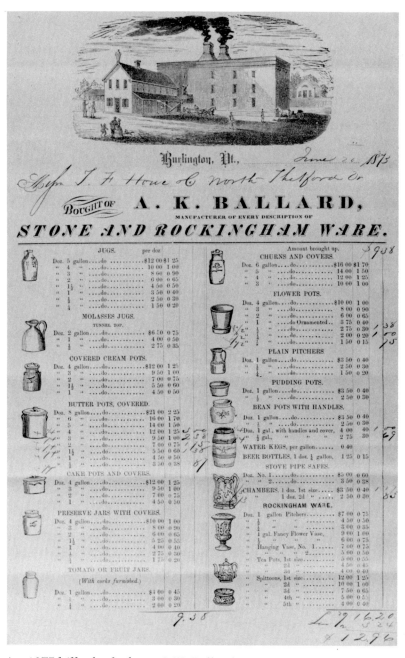

An 1875 bill of sale from A.K. Ballard, a company in Burlington, Vermont, which produced stone and Rockingham ware.

Handles were applied to mugs, pitchers, jars, and similar pieces after the body was formed. The simplest way of forming a handle was by a method known as pulling. A piece of clay was pulled by hand until it resembled either a flat or round rod. This rod was then cut into lengths appropriate for individual handles. These crude handles were applied to the body of the piece. The other method, which made a more decorative handle required the use of an extruder, a tool similar to a hypodermic syringe with a template. The cylinder was filled with clay. As the plunge was depressed, clay was forced through the template to form a length of handle. This formed length of handle was then cut into individual sizes. The spouts on pitchers were either separately formed and attached to the piece or formed by pinching the rim of the pitcher until a crude spout was formed. If a potter marked his ware by impressing or embossing his logo, it was done at this time. After this work was completed, the piece was put in a drying room. It was very important that the piece not have a high water content because firing would turn the water to steam and cause a blow out. As time progressed, the potter's wheel was replaced by molds. Cast or molded pieces were made in one of two ways. The first involved pouring slip, which is liquid clay, into a plaster mold. Plaster was used because it readily absorbs water and, thus, hastens the drying process. When a sufficient thickness of slip had dried and adhered to the wall of the mold, the remaining slip was poured out. Once the piece had thoroughly hardened, it was removed from the mold. If handles, spouts, or other decorations were to be added, it was done at this time using the same method discussed under thrown pieces. The other method involved pressing or forcing clay, into a plaster mold. Once the clay was in place, it was allowed to harden before being removed from the mold. Cast and molded pieces had to be stored in a drying room to reduce their water content. Pie plates and similar pieces were often made by a process known as drape molding. In this process, a piece of clay was rolled flat, then cut into the desired shape, and draped over a mold made of either plaster, clay, or wood. The clay would assume the shape of the mold and, in time, harden. Once the piece hardened, it was smoothed with a wet sponge and removed from the mold.

Decoration

Before discussing the various types of decoration that was applied to yellow ware, Rockingham, Benningtion, and mocha needed to be discussed because of the confusion that surrounds them.

The words Rockingham and Bennington have been used interchangeably to describe a type of decoration. This is incorrect. Rockingham is a type of decoration that was applied to yellow ware; Bennington is a town in Vermont where yellow ware was produced. At Bennington, as well as other potteries throughout the United States, Rockingham decorated yellow ware was produced.

Because of a jargon unique to dealers and collectors, the use of the term mocha has caused confusion. Mocha is a form of decoration; it is not a ware. Thus, one collects a certain type of ware such as yellow ware which is mocha decorated, i. e. mocha decorated yellow ware. However, dealers and collectors who say they deal in or collect mocha usually mean mocha decorated creamware, pearlware, or white earthenware. This is incorrect but has become ingrained in the jargon of the trade.

The following are the types of decoration that can be found on yellow ware:

Plain

After the first firing a clear alkaline-based glaze, which was a mixture of flint, kaolin, and white lead, was applied to the piece. A second firing affixed this glaze to the piece and produced a glossy, glass-like surface.

Banded

Banding, which can consist of one horizontal band to many horizontal bands of the same or different colors, is the most common form of decoration. A slip cup, a vessel containing one or more spouts, was used to dribble slip on a piece as it turned on a potter's wheel or lathe.

Slip is a creamy substance made from clay and water which can have coloring agents added to it. By adding iron oxide, a brownish color was created; cobalt produced a blue color; and chromoxide produced green. Slip was added to a piece before the first firing.

Rockingham

This form of decoration was created by applying a manganese brown glaze to a piece which had gone through its first firing. The glaze was dripped onto the piece to create a mottled or tortoiseshell effect.

Mocha

Before a piece went through the first firing, a wide band of white slip was applied. Then, a mixture or "tea" was dribbled on or touched to the band. Through capillary action, the mixture spread over the slip to form patterns known as tree, thistle, seaweed, moss, and fern. This "tea" was a mixture of ingredients such as hops, turpentine, citric acid, tobacco juice, and stale urine. Mocha decorations known as cat's eye and earthworm were applied in a different manner.

To produce the cat's eye decoration, which is a sphere usually containing three colors, a three chambered slip cup was used to simultaneously drop the colors on the piece. The piece was turned slowly on a lathe so that the slip could be dropped on the piece and produce a distinct tri-colored sphere. To produce the earthworm decoration, the lathe was turned faster so that the colors would run together. If a looped earthworm pattern was desired, the slip cup was moved in a circular motion.

Sponging

Sponging is a decoration achieved by the repetition of a design, usually a circle, oval, "T," rectangle, "L," or square over the entire piece. The design was applied with a stamp or applicator which was soaked in colored slip and then repeatedly touched to the piece. On some pieces, the design is very clear; on others, it is blurred. One or more colors could be used to produce the design.

Flint Enamel

Except for the presence of blue, yellow, black, and green colors, this decoration is very similar to Rockingham because of the heavy use of brown. After the first firing, clear glaze was applied to the piece. Then, oxides were sprinkled on it. During the second firing, the oxides fused with the glaze to produce a flowing brown pattern with a combination of either blue, black, yellow, or green highlights. The method of applying the decoration, not the actual type of decoration, was patented by Christopher Fenton of Bennington, Vermont, in 1849.

Advertising

Although advertising may not be considered a form of decoration by some, it is placed here for convenience. Food producers, manufacturers, restaurants, grocery stores, and other retail operations used yellow ware as a medium for their message. These pieces were either free, given away as a premium, or were packaging for food. The message, which was stenciled or stamped on the piece, could simply be the name of the retailer or a message extolling the virtues of the product or service. Bowls, crocks, pie plates, rolling pins, pitchers, and beater jars carried these messages.

Firing

If the firing was done improperly, all the work done to this point would have been in vain. The kiln had to be fired correctly or several problems could occur. If the temperature rose too quickly, the remaining moisture in a piece could turn to steam and cause a blow-out or the piece could expand too quickly and crack. When the desired temperature was reached, it had to be maintained. If the temperature rose too far above this point, the piece would begin to sag and then liquify.

The kiln was composed of two parts: a firebox and a chamber in which the pieces were placed. A beehive-shaped chamber was the most efficient because it eliminated cold spots. When pieces were stacked in the chamber, they had to be properly supported and correctly exposed to the heat. Usually, two pieces were used to support one piece and plates were stacked on end in rows. Because gas-fired kilns did not come into use before the last quarter of the 19th century, wood was used in the firebox to produce the desired temperature. Hardwood was preferred because it burned longer and cleaner than softwood.

Once the first firing was completed and the cooled pieces removed from the kiln, glaze was applied to them. Then, the pieces were restacked in the kiln for the second or gloss firing. Not only did the pieces have to be properly supported but they could not touch. The glaze would fuse the pieces together. Objects known as coils, trivets, and stilts were used to separate the pieces. Stilt marks, which are tiny unglazed areas, can be found on some pieces, especially pie plates. When the second firing was finished and the pieces had cooled, they were removed from the kiln. They were now ready to be sold.

Attribution

This topic is placed at the end of this section because it should be of least concern to a collector who wants to amass a representative collection of yellow ware. Some collectors become overly concerned with a piece's country of origin: the United States, Canada, Great Britain, or Europe. If an individual wants to collect pieces that were made in the United States, the collection will be limited to pieces which are marked and to those pieces which research has shown were produced only in the United States. Examples of the latter would be pipkins, washboards, and canister sets. Over the years theories which supposedly prove the country of origin have evolved. The best that can be said about these claims is that they can provide a strong hint, perhaps an educated guess, as to the country of origin, but cannot provide definite proof. Because a collector will encounter these theories, the major ones and their exceptions are noted.

1. If a piece produces a clear ring when it is tapped, it was made in Great Britain. If the sound is dull, it was made in the United States. By testing marked pieces, one will discover that the reverse is also true. Thus, definite attribution is impossible.

2. Pieces made in Great Britain have thinner walls and better defined detail than those made in the United States. On average, this statement is correct but not all the time. To make this theory the basis for definite attribution, it would have to be correct all the time. It is not.

3. Pieces, such as bowls and nappies, which have a white interior were made in Great Britain. More often than not this statement is correct. However, companies in the United States, especially in Ohio and Pennsylvania, also produced pieces with white interiors. These were considered, for a short time, to be more sanitary than the yellow interior usually seen.

4. Mugs and cups made in Great Britain had fancier handles (called foliated, a leaf-like design) than their American counterparts. Again on average, this is correct. However, it is not always correct.

5. The colors used to decorate a piece can aid in determining the country of origin. It is commonly believed that pieces decorated with three colors of mocha were only made in Great Britain. Because there is no evidence as yet that a similar tricolored decoration was used in the United States, this is correct. However, the use of certain colors or combination of colors cannot be used in any other instance to definitely determine the country of origin.

In conclusion, if a piece is marked or research has shown that it was produced only in the United States, definite attribution can be made. If this is not the case, one can, after handling many pieces, make an educated guess as to the country of origin. However, if one is sincere about building a serious collection, the question should not be the country of origin but if a piece fills a void or complements others pieces in the collection.

Part II:

THE MANUFACTURERS

Over the years, researchers have uncovered the existence of hundreds of individuals and companies involved in the production of yellow ware. Except for a select few, most of them made no important contribution to the field. Not much more than their names, ownership, and dates of operation are known. If available, price lists and catalogs provide a clue as to what was produced. These lists can be misleading because there was no standard terminology and some companies which listed yellow ware acted as only retail or wholesale distributors. Although some of the companies made creative contributions such as mocha decorated colanders and teapots, melon tureens, and doorstops, none of them made any technological contributions. This presentation is limited to companies that had a creative impact on the field and a select few which were representative of a typical operation.

The events which took place during the rise and fall of yellow ware closely reflect what happens in other industries. Large companies drove smaller ones out of business. Expanding transportation systems made raw materials more accessible and opened new markets for finished goods. New technologies, such as gas-fired kilns, not only facilitated production but made the cost of entry into the field more prohibitive. Creativity, a driving force during the industry's infancy, gave way to mass production and homogeneity. And, changing consumer tastes brought an era to an end.

Potters were a transient group. The exceptional group of potters and modelers that David Henderson assembled in Jersey City, New Jersey, soon spread throughout the state and to locations in Ohio, Pennsylvania, Vermont, and Maryland. Whether these individuals were entrepreneurial, restless, or a combination of both we will never know. Their contribution was to spread knowledge and skill throughout the industry. Potteries came in all sizes. For some, it was a cottage industry used to supplement their incomes. These potteries depended on the local availability of clay and local markets to sustain their operations. As technology advanced and improved, transportation systems opened new markets to large companies, and the existence of these "mom and pop" potteries became tenuous. As mass production became the keystone of the industry, creativity faded from the scene. However, given the nature and use of this ware, could creativity continue to be a driving force? On a positive note, new forms were introduced in the 20th century and certain forms did take on an Art Deco appearance. By this time, though, the yellow ware industry was in decline.

The East

Although New York and Pennsylvania can lay claim to having the first yellow ware potteries, the responsibility fell to New Jersey to take the creative lead in the production of yellow ware. In 1824, David Henderson, a Scot, together with George Drummer, purchased the assets of the defunct Jersey Pottery and Porcelain Works in Jersey City to manufacture porcelain. The venture was unsuccessful and Henderson purchased the firm's assets from his partner in 1828. Henderson's brother, James, joined the firm which had ceased the production of porcelain in favor of yellow ware, Rockingham, and stoneware. Their pieces bear the impressed mark "D&J HENDERSON/JERSEY CITY" or "D&J HENDERSON/1829" in a circle. In 1833, the company changed its name to the American Pottery Manufacturing Company. In 1840, the company's name was again changed to the American Pottery Company. This new name necessitated a change in the impressed mark to "AMERICAN/POTTERY CO./JERSEY CITY, NJ" in a circle. Impressed numbers, 0, 000, 1, 2, 3, 4, or 5 were also in the circle. It is believed that the company stopped producing yellow ware around 1839-40 to concentrate on the production of whiteware. In 1859, the company was sold.

Henderson's greatest contribution was to employ the most skilled potters and modelers in the industry. These individuals produced outstanding molds which would be used to speed the production process. The most noteworthy of these individuals were Daniel Greatbach and James Bennett. Greatbach is credited with crafting the hound handled pitcher and many of the molds the company used. Neither of these accomplishments were original but had a great impact on domestic yellow ware production. Hound handled pitchers had already been produced in Great Britain. However, Greatbach refined the design to a level that was previously unknown. Molds had been previously used in the production of wares in both Great Britain and the United States. The use of molds to produce yellow ware made mass production possible. Signaling the obsolescence of the potter's wheel, this development meant that semi-skilled workers could produce more pieces in less time with fewer mistakes. This lowered the cost of goods and made domestically produced yellow ware more attractive to consumers.

James Bennett, who migrated from South Derbyshire, England, in 1834, was another creative potter and modeler in Henderson's employ. Bennett's tenure at Henderson's operation lasted approximately three years. After working in Troy, Indiana, and Cincinnati, Ohio, he arrived in East Liverpool and established the city's first pottery in 1840. To aid in this venture, Bennett's brothers, William, Daniel, and Edwin, joined him. Despite the creative and managerial talents of the Bennetts, the pottery closed its doors in 1844. Edwin and William moved to Pittsburgh, Pennsylvania, and established the Pennsylvania Pottery. In 1846, Edwin moved to Baltimore, Maryland and established Edwin Bennett & Co. William soon joined him in this venture. Remaining active till 1918 the pottery used several impressed marks: "E.&W. BENNETT / CANTON AVENUE / BALTIMORE, MD.", "E. BENNETT / BALTIMORE, MD.", and "E. BENNETT'S / PATENT/ DEC. 2, 1853."

Because of the abundance of clay and the proximity to large markets, a large number of potteries were established in New Jersey. The most important ones were:

SOUTH AMBOY: John Hancock: 1828-1840
Congress Hill Pottery: 1849-1854
Swan Hill Pottery: 1849-1871

PERTH AMBOY: Eagle Pottery: 1858-1865
Alfred Hall & Sons: 1866-1880

WOODBRIDGE: Salamander Works: 1825-1896

TRENTON: Trenton Pottery: 1852-1878
Glasgow Pottery Co: 1863-1900
Excelsior Pottery: 1857-1880
William H. Young: 1853-1857
Carol Street Pottery: 1852-1857

Pennsylvania was another major center for the production of yellow ware. Although there is controversy as to whether or not John Mullowny produced true yellow ware, his Washington Pottery (1809-1816) is given credit with being the first to produce yellow ware in the state. Given the lack of material to validate what was produced at this Philadelphia pottery and its short existence, the J.E. Jeffords Company (1868-1904) is the best known of the Keystone State's potteries. This notoriety is aided by the fact that the Jeffords mark is the most common of all marks found on domestically produced yellow ware. Two marks have been credited to Jeffords: an impressed mark and a blue stamp which is the later of the two. Although the pottery existed until 1904 and was awarded a medal for its yellow ware at the Philadelphia Centennial Exposition (1876), the company began to concentrate on the production of whitewares in the mid 1870s. This change of emphasis is similar to what happened at many potteries. Although they originally concentrated on the production of yellow ware, changing consumer tastes necessitated that other wares be put in production. Thus, although a pottery may have remained in existence for 50 years, it did not necessarily produce yellow ware for the entire period.

Yellow Rock, a pottery in Philadelphia, remains a mystery to researchers. Pipkins, nappies, and mini-molds have been found with the company's mark; a blue or black stamped circle containing the words, "YELLOW ROCK, PHILA." Because some researchers believe that mini-molds are a late form, they have assumed that the pottery was in operation during the 20th century. However, physical evidence such as tax records, advertisements, and citations in city directories does not exist. Given the supposed time of operation, this situation is very difficult to explain. Other researchers contend that Yellow Rock was one of the earliest potteries because more marked pieces from J.E. Jeffords exist and some of the pieces produced by Jeffords are exactly like those produced by Yellow Rock. These researchers feel that mini-molds are an early form and that Yellow Rock closed and sold its molds to Jeffords. This debate will not be settled until dated physical evidence is found.

Other Philadelphia area potteries which deserve mention are:

PHILADELPHIA: Thomas Haig: 1812-1890
                        Spring Garden Pottery: 1840-1851

PHOENIXVILLE: The Phoenix Pottery: 1867-1879

One of the most well known Pennsylvania potters was John Bell. Bell, who began his career in Maryland, established a pottery in Waynesboro in 1833. Best known for his redware, Bell produced a very limited line of yellow ware until 1880. Bell marked his pieces with an impressed "JOHN BELL" or "JOHN BELL/WAYNESBORO."

Although Pittsburgh was one of the industrial and population centers of Pennsylvania, the area is not noted for producing a significant amount of yellow ware. As previously mentioned, Edwin and William Bennett established the Pennsylvania Pottery. The only other pottery of any consequence was run by Jabez Vodrey. However, this pottery remained in operation for only three years (1827-1830).

In the state of New York, Syracuse was the center of yellow ware production. However, because of the emphasis on stoneware, the production of yellow ware was very limited. The Syracuse potteries which produced, not distributed, yellow ware were Manchester & Clark, the Syracuse Stoneware Company, and the Furnace Street Pottery. In Utica, The White Pottery Company, also known as White's Utica, produced a very limited line for a short period of time. The New York City Pottery as well as Otto Lewis, Mechanicville, New York, did the same.

Little is presently known about the production of yellow ware in Delaware. In Hockessin, Abner Marshall operated a pottery from 1859-1866 which produced both plain and Rockingham decorated yellow ware. Although there may have been other potteries in the state, their names have not come to light.

The South

Except for Maryland, the South produced very little yellow ware. In Maryland, two companies, the Chesapeake Pottery (1879-1882) and Edwin Bennett & Co., produced yellow ware. As previously mentioned, Bennett had worked at his brother's pottery in East Liverpool, Ohio. After a short stay in Pittsburgh, Pennsylvania, he moved to Baltimore, and established a pottery. Although this business continued into the 20th century, the 1870s marked the decline of its yellow ware production.

In South Carolina, the Southern Porcelain Company (or Southern Pottery Company) produced some yellow ware. In 1856, William H. Farrer, a former shareholder in the U.S. Pottery Co. of Bennington, Vermont, moved to Kaolin, South Carolina and established the Southern Porcelain Company. Despite a rocky financial start, the pottery remained open until 1865. The plain and Rockingham decorated yellow ware forms produced by the company were

An 1898 bill of sales from the Syracuse Stoneware Company.

marked S.P.C., S.P. Company, or "FIRE PROOF SPCo." The Lewis Pottery Co. (1829-1837) in Louisville, Kentucky, produced a limited line of yellow ware. In 1837, James Clews, who managed the potteries in Cambridge, England, moved to Troy, Indiana and established The Indiana Pottery to produce porcelain and white ware. When this company was incorporated it absorbed The Lewis Pottery Co.

New England

Bennington, Vermont, was the main producer of yellow ware in New England. A growing population, a seemingly endless supply of wood, and easy accessibility to transportation systems made this town an ideal location. Although the amount of yellow ware produced was massive, the majority of it was decorated with either Rockingham or flint enamel glaze. Thus, yellow ware as it is traditionally collected falls outside the majority of what was produced at Bennington. Rockingham and flint enamel glazed yellow ware is usually, but not always, a separate collecting field. Some of the best designed pieces of yellow ware came from Bennington. A hound handled pitcher produced here was superior to similar ones produced both here and abroad. It is an interesting twist of fate that Daniel Greatbach who modeled this pitcher had previously modeled the same but less sophisticated form for David Henderson. In addition to finely detailed figurals such as cow creamers, inkwells, and paperweights, a full line of pieces was produced.

The history of yellow ware production in Bennington revolves around the names Norton and Fenton. These two families were drawn together by marriage and a short-lived business partnership. Arriving in Bennington during 1793, John Norton purchased a farm and established a pottery, distillery, and blacksmith shop. Norton had two sons, Lyman and John Jr., who were brought into the pottery business. However, John Jr. soon disassociated himself from the business to pursue othe interests. Lyman's marriage produced a son, Julius, who entered the business, and a daughter, Louisa. In 1832, Louisa married Christopher Fenton, the son of Jonathan Fenton. Although Jonathan was not the first Fenton to establish a pottery in Vermont, he was the most successful. In 1801, he built a kiln in Dorset. Nine years later, he moved the business to East Dorset. Although far from the truth, it was said that Fenton sold to persons living north of Dorset and Norton sold to everyone living south of the town.

In 1844, Julius Norton and Christopher Fenton entered into a partnership. Given the nature of these two individuals, the partnership was destined to fail. Norton was content to produce stoneware, yellow ware, and Rockingham. In addition to these wares, Fenton wanted to produce porcelain. Norton's sole interest was the pottery. Fenton divided his time between the pottery, a dry goods store, and a powder company. When the partnership dissolved, Fenton took on two partners and formed Lyman, Fenton, and Park (1847-1849). In 1849, Park left the partnership; Fenton and Lyman formed The United States Pottery Company (1849-1858). The company produced yellow ware, Rockingham, and porcelain. From the start, the rising cost of raw materials, an abnormally high breakage rate, and an increase in delinquent accounts made for a very tenuous financial existence. Although Fenton is considered the greatest potter of his times, this skill was not enough to overcome the company's worsening financial situation. In 1858, he dissolved the partnership and moved to Peoria, Illinois. From 1858 to early 1859, the pottery continued in operation under the name of A.A. Gilbert & Co. In September of 1859, the workers at the pottery pooled their limited resources and formed the New England Pottery Company. However, this reorganization collapsed in January of 1860. Despite these two reorganizations, Fenton's move to Peoria marked the end of any significant yellow ware production in Vermont. Although Nicholas & Co. (1854-1860) and A.K. Ballard & Co. (1856-1872), both of Burlington, produced Rockingham, they did not manufacture yellow ware.

After the 1847 split with Fenton, Julius Norton continued the family business but production was centered around stoneware. Through a succession of family members, the Nortons retained control of the pottery until 1883. In that year, Edward Norton, the son of John Norton Jr., had to obtain outside financing. Edward Norton died in 1885 and his son, also named Edward, took over the family interests. Around this time, the sale of stoneware began to falter. The company took on other lines as both a producer and distributor. Continuing financial problems forced the pottery to close in 1914. However, Edward Norton, who was the last family member involved in the business, died in 1894. It is ironic that this year also marked the end of stoneware production at the pottery. Yellow ware production was very minimal in other New England states. Except for some cottage industry type operations, Maine did not have one major pottery producing yellow ware. Those companies which listed yellow ware were acting as retail and wholesale agents. New Hampshire could boast of only one major company, The Manchester Pottery Works, which actually produced the ware. In Massachusetts, the Boston Earthenware Factory, the New England Pottery Company, and the Somerset Pottery produced limited lines of yellow ware. All of these companies were located in Boston. No evidence has come to light to substantiate the production of yellow ware in Rhode Island. In Connecticut, George Waters in Stamford and Abalone Day in Norwalk operated potteries that produced a very limited line of yellow ware. Items from Waters pottery can be found marked "GEO. WATERS/STAMFORD, CT./FIREPROOF." Although pieces from the Day Pottery are not marked, it is considered the more important operation. In 1793, Day established the pottery and operated it until 1831. In that year, he turned the operation over to his two sons, George and Noah, who kept the pottery open until 1834. The pottery was then leased to William Taylor who ceased the production of yellow ware. In 1825, Asa E. Smith, a nephew of Abalone Day's wife, opened a pottery in Norwalk. This pottery also produced some yellow ware. Smith went through a series of partners until his sons joined the firm in 1843. In 1874, Asa died and the firm became A.E. Smith's Sons Pottery Co. The firm remained in the family until it was sold to the Norwalk Pottery Co. in 1887.

Ohio

In terms of both the number of potteries and the sheer number of pieces produced, Ohio must definitely be considered the yellow ware capital of the United States. Although the abundance of clay and natural gas, good transportation systems, and expanding markets made the state an ideal location, success was not guaranteed. Natural disasters, intense competition, a Civil War, and periodic recessions spelled disaster for many companies. The worst case of intense competition and market saturation is provided by East Liverpool which had more than 40 potters. Plus, it was only one of four pottery producing centers in the state. The other locations were Cincinnati, Roseville, and Zanesville. And from 1840 until 1872, yellow ware and Rockingham were the sole products of these East Liverpool potters. In 1861 and 1862, William Bloor produced whiteware but financial problems forced the closure of his East Liverpool Porcelain Works. The fragile, sometimes quirky, existence of potteries is best exemplified by the fortunes of James Bennett, Benjamin Harker, and John Goodwin.

As previously mentioned, James Bennett, who worked for David Henderson in New Jersey, is credited with starting the first yellow ware pottery in East Liverpool. Pieces produced at his pottery were impressed BENNETT & BROTHERS/LIVERPOOL, OHIO or had an impressed mark which resembled a four leaf clover. Although Bennett was a skilled potter and an astute businessman, economic hard times forced him to close the pottery within four years (1840-1844). These assets were sold to Thomas Croxall. Together with his father and brothers, he ran the Croxall Pottery until it was destroyed by fire in 1852. Four years later, he opened the Union Pottery. Under various company names and with a constantly changing group of financial backers, the Croxall family managed to run the pottery until they sold it in 1914.

In 1840, Beniamin Harker, Sr. established the second pottery in East Liverpool. Probably due to the fact that Harker wasn't a potter, the business closed within a year. Between 1841 and 1845, Harker leased the kiln to two different groups of potters. Both of these ventures failed within a year of opening. Throwing caution to the wind, Harker and his two sons, Benjamin, Jr. and George, reopened the pottery. In 1846, John Taylor entered the firm and it was renamed Harker, Taylor, & Co. A new three-story pottery was constructed and named Etruria. Although the firm produced a variety of wares including Rockingham, it did not produce yellow ware until 1851. This date also marks the beginning of a series of partnerships which were periodically necessary to provide operating capital. In 1853, Benjamin Harker, Jr. left the firm and purchased the former Mansion House Pottery with William Smith. The firm, which produced yellow ware and Rockingham, was forced to close in 1855. Benjamin returned to the Etruria Pottery until 1877 when he and his sons established the Wedgewood Pottery. W.W. Harker, George Harker's son, took over the management of the firm. In 1879, the production of yellow ware was stopped in favor of manufacturing white ironstone. The firm continued to exist until 1972.

John Goodwin was another interesting character who produced yellow ware in East Liverpool. Goodwin was in the pottery business for 26 years. However, these were not continuous years. After working for James Bennett and Peter Harker, Goodwin established the Eagle Pottery in 1843 and sold it in 1853. It was not until 1863 that he started the Novelty Pottery Co. which remained open until 1865. In 1870 he turned up in Trenton, New Jersey, as one of the partners in the Trenton Pottery Company. Two years later, he returned to East Liverpool and, together with his sons, founded John Goodwin & Sons. The pottery retained that name until 1875, the year Goodwin died. His sons reorganized the company under the name of Goodwin Brothers Pottery and discontinued the production of yellow ware. The pottery finally closed its doors in 1913.

The stories of these individuals are representative of the fortunes of most of the potters in Ohio. Skill and good business sense alone did not guarantee success. Longevity, an illusive goal for most, usually depended on periodic cash infusions from backers and diversifying into other lines. Because yellow ware serviced a particular and limited customer need, potters did not nor could not stray from this niche. Thus, with few exceptions, the same pieces were produced by every pottery. As the 20th century neared, most potteries had to diversify their offerings to stay solvent. For example, whiteware was becoming very popular. Companies were forced to

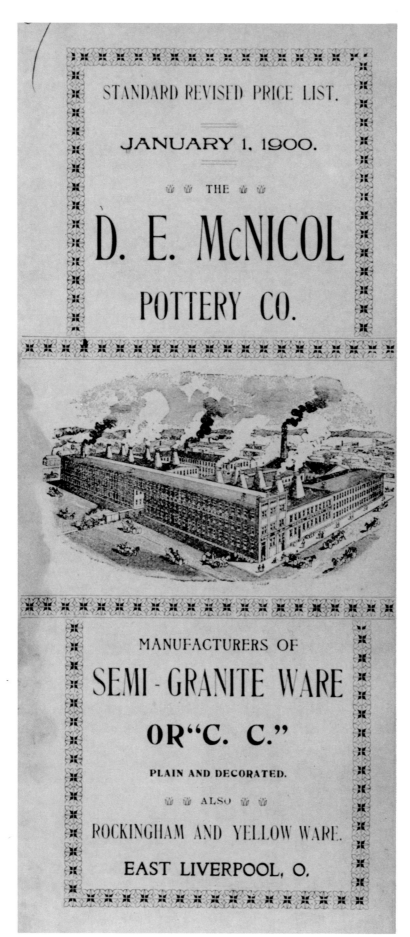

STANDARD REVISED PRICE LIST.

JANUARY 1, 1900.

THE

D. E. McNICOL

POTTERY CO.

MANUFACTURERS OF

SEMI - GRANITE WARE

OR "C. C."

PLAIN AND DECORATED.

ALSO

ROCKINGHAM AND YELLOW WARE.

EAST LIVERPOOL, O.

Pages 20 through 23 show a price list of the D.E. McNicol Pottery Co. of East Liverpool, Ohio.

JUGS, Granite Shape, Self Rock.

36s, 1 pint	$1 00
30s, 1¼ pints	1 25
24s, 2¾ pints	1 75
12s, 4 pints	3 00
6s, 6 pints	4 50
4s, 8 pints	6 00

ALE JUGS.

1s, 8 pints	$10 00
2s, 6 pints	8 00

MUGS.

36s, ½ pint	$ 55
30s, ¾ pint	65
24s, 1 pint	75

NAPPIES, Round.

2-inch, diameter 4-inch	$ 55
3-inch, diameter 5-inch	60
4-inch, diameter 5⅝-inch	65
5-inch, diameter 6⅝-inch	75
6-inch, diameter 7⅝-inch	90
7-inch, diameter 8⅝-inch	1 10
8-inch, diameter 9½-inch	1 35
9-inch, diameter 10⅜-inch	1 65
10-inch, diameter 11¼-inch	2 10
11-inch, diameter 12-inch	3 25
12-inch, diameter 13-inch	3 25
13-inch, diameter 14-inch	4 20

MILK OR CAKE PANS.

12s, diameter 190-inch	$1 75
9s, diameter 11¼-inch	2 50
6s, diameter 12-inch	3 25
4s, diameter 13-inch	4 50

ROCK MILK BOILERS.

1½ pints	$1 25
2 pints	1 50
3 pints	1 80
4 pints	2 20

BAKERS, Oval.

Per doz.

6-inch, diameter 7-inch	$ 85
7-inch, diameter 8-inch	1 05
8-inch, diameter 9-inch	1 25
9-inch, diameter 10-inch	1 55
10-inch, diameter 11-inch	1 85
11-inch, diameter 12-inch	2 30
12-inch, diameter 13-inch	2 80

BAKERS, Square, New Shape.

6-inch, diameter 7-inch	$1 00
7-inch, diameter 8-inch	1 25
8-inch, diameter 9-inch	1 60
9-inch, diameter 10-inch	2 00
10-inch, diameter 11-inch	2 40
11-inch, diameter 12-inch	2 80
12-inch, diameter 13-inch	3 50

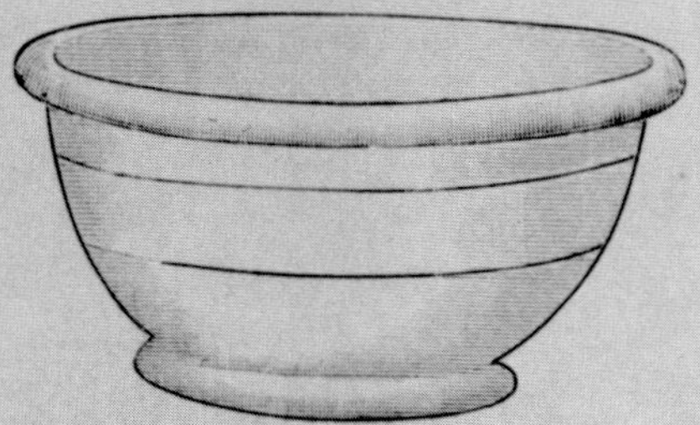

BOWLS, Pressed.

42s, diameter 4½-inch	$ 40
36s, diameter 5¼-inch	50
30s, diameter 6-inch	60
24s, diameter 6⅝-inch	75
18s, diameter 7¾-inch	1 25
12s, diameter 8½-inch	1 60
9s, diameter 10¼-inch	2 25
6s, diameter 11¼-inch	3 25
4s, diameter 12½-inch	4 50
3s, diameter 13½-inch	6 25
2s, diameter 14½-inch	9 00
1s, diameter 15½-inch	14 00

BUTTER JARS, Covered.

12s, 1¼ quarts	$2 50
9s, 2 quarts	3 75
6s, 3 quarts	5 00
4s, 4 quarts	6 50

BED PANS, French.

No. 1, large	$9 00

CHAMBERS, Open.

12s diameter 7⅛-inch	$2 00
9s, diameter 8¼-inch	2 75
6s, diameter 9⅛-inch	3 50
4s, diameter 10-inch	4 50

Covers Half Price.

SPITTOONS, Mammoth.

Diameter 14 inch $12 00

SPITTOONS, Plain Top.

Per doz.

5s, diameter 7-inch........ ....$2 00
4s, diameter 8-inch 3 00
3s, diameter 9-inch 4 00
2s, diameter 10-inch 5 00
1s, diameter 11¼-inch 6 00

PIE PLATES.

7-inch, diameter 8¼-inch 75
8-inch, diameter 9¼-inch 85
9-inch, diameter 10⅛-inch 95
10-inch, diameter 11-inch 1 05

SOAP DRAINERS.

1s, oval, 5½-inch $1 50
2s, oval, 4¾-inch 1 25
1s, kitchen soap 2 00

TEA POTS, Large Size.
Pineapple, Chinaman, Rebecca and Columbia.

Individual or Old Maid............$2 00
48s, 1 pint 2 20
42s, 2 pints 2 40
36s, 2½ pints 2 65
30s, 3¼ pints 3 00
24s, 4 pints 3 50
18s, 5¼ pints 4 25
12s, 7 pints 5 50
9s, 8½ pints 6 50

BAKERS, Oval.

Per doz.

6-inch, diameter 7-inch ....$ 75
7-inch, diameter 8-inch 90
8-inch, diameter 9-inch 1 10
9-inch, diameter 10-inch 1 40
10-inch, diameter 11 inch 1 70
11-inch, diameter 11-inch 2 00
12-inch, diameter 13-inch 2 50

BAKERS, Square, New Shape.

6-inch, diameter 7-inch ....$ 75
7-inch, diameter 8-inch 90
8-inch, diameter 9-inch 1 10
9-inch, diameter 10-inch 1 40
10-inch, diameter 11-inch 1 70
11-inch, diameter 12-inch 2 00
12-inch, diameter 13-inch 2 50
13-inch, diameter 14-inch 3 00

BOWLS.
Round rim, turned and banded.

42s, diameter 4½-inch ....$ 35
36s, diameter 5¼-inch 40
30s, diameter 6-inch 50
24s, diameter 6⅜-inch 60
18s, diameter 7¾-inch 1 10
12s, diameter 8½-inch 1 50
9s, diameter 10¼-inch 2 00
6s, diameter 11¼-inch 3 00
4s, diameter 12½-inch 4 25
3s, diameter 13½-inch 5 75
2s, diameter 14½-inch 8 00
1s, diameter 15½-inch ....)12 00

BOWLS, Pressed, Heavy Rim.

18s, diameter 7¾-inch $1 10
12s, diameter 8½-inch 1 50
9s, diameter 10¼-inch 2 00
6s, diameter 11¼-inch 3 00
4s, diameter 12½-inch 4 25

BUTTER JARS—Covered.

12s, 2½ pints $2 25
9s, 4 pints 3 25
6s, 6 pints 4 50
4s, 8 pints 6 00

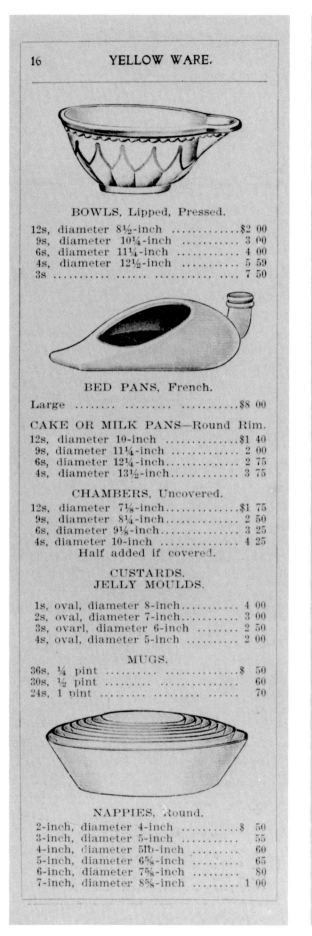

BOWLS, Lipped, Pressed.

12s, diameter 8½-inch $2 00
9s, diameter 10¼-inch 3 00
6s, diameter 11¼-inch 4 00
4s, diameter 12½-inch 5 59
3s 7 50

BED PANS, French.

Large $8 00

CAKE OR MILK PANS—Round Rim.
12s, diameter 10-inch $1 40
9s, diameter 11¼-inch 2 00
6s, diameter 12¼-inch............. 2 75
4s, diameter 13½-inch............. 3 75

CHAMBERS, Uncovered.
12s, diameter 7⅛-inch.............$1 75
9s, diameter 8¼-inch............. 2 50
6s, diameter 9⅛-inch............. 3 25
4s, diameter 10-inch 4 25
Half added if covered.

CUSTARDS.
JELLY MOULDS.

1s, oval, diameter 8-inch.......... 4 00
2s, oval, diameter 7-inch.......... 3 00
3s, ovarl, diameter 6-inch 2 50
4s, oval, diameter 5-inch 2 00

MUGS.
36s, ¼ pint ....$ 50
30s, ½ pint 60
24s, 1 pint 70

NAPPIES, Round.
2-inch, diameter 4-inch ....$ 50
3-inch, diameter 5-inch 55
4-inch, diameter 5lb-inch 60
5-inch, diameter 6¾-inch 65
6-inch, diameter 7⅝-inch 80
7-inch, diameter 8⅝-inch 1 00

8-inch, diameter 9½-inch 1 20
9-inch, diameter 10⅛-inch........ 1 50
10-inch, diameter 11¼-inch........ 1 90
11-inch, diameter 12-inch 2 40
12-inch, diameter 13-inch 3 00
13-inch, diameter 14-inch.......... 3 20

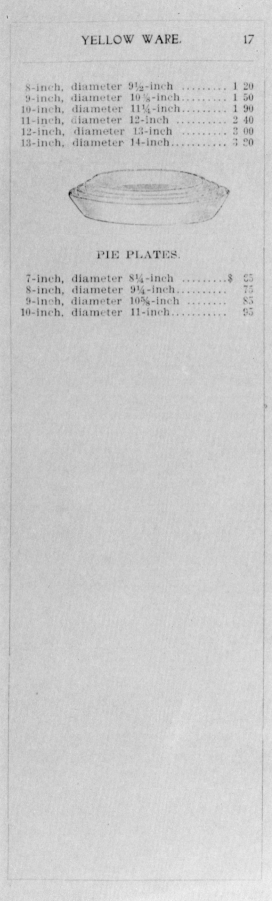

PIE PLATES.

7-inch, diameter 8¼-inch ....$ 65
8-inch, diameter 9¼-inch.......... 75
9-inch, diameter 10⅝-inch 85
10-inch, diameter 11-inch.......... 95

produce both wares or to drop yellow ware. This change in production priorities did not mean that yellow ware production stopped shortly after the beginning of the 20th century. Production began to fall off but continued on a small scale until the 1940s.

In addition to the potteries already discussed, the following deserve mention:

EAST LIVERPOOL: Salt & Mear (1842-1850)
                The American Pottery (1863-1881)
                Star Pottery (1875-1888)

CINCINNATI: Berlin Street Pottery (1871-1895)
            Uriah Kendall & Sons (1839-1870)
            Vine Street Pottery (1859-1880)

ZANESVILLE: Tremont Pottery (1879-1900)

The West

West of Ohio, few yellow ware potteries were established because of the distance from raw materials, smaller markets, and poorer transportation systems. Christopher Fenton and Daniel Greatbach established a short lived operation in Peoria, Illinois. A.M. Johnson also operated the American Pottery (1864-1873) in Peoria. The Morton Pottery Company in Morton, Illinois, produced a small line of yellow ware. The Red Wing Stoneware Co. in Red Wing, Minnesota, also produced a limited line which was marketed under the name of Saffron Ware. After a merger and reorganization, the company was known as the Red Wing Potteries. And in Ripley, Illinois, John N. Stout operated a pottery from 1866 to 1887 which produced some yellow ware. Other potteries were located in Missouri and Indiana. In Cape Girardeau, Missouri, James Post operated a pottery (1881-1885) which produced a limited line of yellow ware. As previously mentioned, James Clews established The Indiana Pottery in Troy, Indiana, to produce porcelain and white ware. Because of the poor quality of the clay and the lack of skilled workers, the pottery soon found itself on shaky financial ground. To improve its financial health, the pottery began to produce yellow ware and Rockingham. Jabez Vodrey was brought in to run the pottery in 1839 and Clews returned to England. The pottery remained open until 1846. In 1851, John Sanders and Samuel Wilson reopened the pottery. Four years later, Sanders bought out Wilson and kept the pottery open until 1863. In that year, Benjamin Hinchco leased the pottery and kept it running for the next 20 years. At that time, the pottery closed its doors forever. In Brazil, Indiana, Isaac Cordrey (1868-1869) and Tourpart & Baker (1859-1890) produced some yellow ware.

In the far West, The Pioneer Pottery (1856-1887) in East Oakland, California produced a line of yellow ware. In Los Angeles, the Pacific Clay Manufacturing Company (1884-1910) and J.A. Bauer & Company (1890-1959) produced yellow ware. Both of these companies marked their pieces.

Manufacturer's Marks

As previously mentioned, not all potters marked the pieces they produced and the potters who marked their pieces did not necessarily mark every piece or form. A potter might mark the pie plates he produced but not the nappies and possibly might not mark all the pie plates. Also, a potter might mark his yellow ware but not his whiteware.

Three types of marks are usually found on yellow ware: impressed, raised, and stamped. A potter usually used only one type of mark. There are exceptions to this rule such as J.E. Jeffords & Co. which used both an impressed mark and a stamp.

This section presents a detailed description of the marks of American potters by state. A short section on Canadian and British marks follows.

MANUFACTURER	DATES	MARK
California Pacific Clay Manufacturing Company, Los Angeles	1880-1930	PACIFIC in elongated diamond, impressed.
J.A. Bauer & Company, Los Angeles	1890-1958	BAUER; stamped
Connecticut Geo. Watson, Stamford	?	GEO. WATSON/STAMFORD/CONN/FIREPROOF; impressed.
Illinois Morton Pottery, Morton	1920-1930	MORTON POTTERY/ILLINOIS; impressed.
Maryland Edwin and William Bennett, Baltimore	1846-1848	E&W BENNETT/CANTON ST/BALTIMORE; impressed.
Edwin Bennett, Baltimore	1848-1875	E. BENNETT/PATENT/DEC. 2, 1853; impressed
Massachusetts Boston Earthenware Manufactory, Boston	1854-1876	BOSTON EARTHEN/WARE/MANUF'G CO; impressed BOSTON/EARTHENWARE FACTORY; impressed.
Minnesota Red Wing Union Stoneware, Red Wing	1933-1936	RED WING/SAFFRON/WARE; stamped.
Red Wing Potteries, Red Wing	1936-1945	RED WING/SAFFRON/WARE; stamped
New Jersey D&J Henderson Jersey City	1829-1833	D&J HENDERSON/JERSEY CITY; impressed in a circle-

MANUFACTURER	DATES	MARK
D&J Henderson (cont.)		D&J HENDERSON; impressed
		HENDERSON'S STONEWARE MANUFACTORY / JERSEY CITY; impressed
American Pottery Company, Jersey City	1833-1857	AMERICAN POTTERY / MANUFACTURING COM-PANY / JERSEY CITY: impressed.
		AMERICAN / POTTERY CO. / JERSEY CITY, N.J.; raised letters in a circle with raised numbers 0, 000, 1, 2, 3, 4, or 5.
		AMERICAN / POTTERY / CO. / JERSEY CITY; raised letters in circle with raised numbers as above.
J.L. Rue Pottery Co., Matawan	1860-1875	J.L. RUE & CO.; raised.
		THE J.L. RUE POTTERY CO. / MATAWAN / N.J.; raised.
Abraham Cadmus Congress Pottery South Amboy	1849-1854	A CADMUS / CONGRESS POTTERY / SOUTH AMBOY / N.J.; impressed
Swan Hill Pottery South Amboy	1849-1860	SWAN HILL / POTTERY / SOUTH AMBOY; impressed.
Edward Hanks and Charles Fish South Amboy	1850-1851	HANKS & FISH / SWAN HILL / POTTERY / S. AMBOY, N. JERSEY; impressed
Salamander Works Woodbridge	1838-1850	SALAMANDER / WORKS / CANNON STREET / NEW YORK; impressed. (The sales office was in New York City.)
I. W. Cory Trenton	1867-1870	I.W. CORY / TRENTON; impressed.
New York Thomas Carr City Pottery, New York	1856-1860	CITY POTTERY / WEST 12TH ST. N.Y.; impressed.

MANUFACTURER	DATES	MARK
Roycroft Shops East Aurora	1915-1925	R; impressed THE ROYCROFT SHOPS/ EAST AURORA/NY; impressed.
Otto V. Lewis Mechanicville	1860-?	OTTO V. LEWIS/MECHAN- ICVILLE; impressed.

Ohio

MANUFACTURER	DATES	MARK
James Bennett Bennett Brothers East Liverpool	1839-1841 1841-1844	BENNETT & BROTHERS/ LIVERPOOL OHIO; impressed Four rounded triangles in a clover design; impressed.
Croxall & Cart- wright East Liverpool	1856-1888	CROXALL & CARTWRIGHT/ EAST/LIVERPOOL/OHIO; raised
Croxall Brothers East Liverpool	1888-1914	CROXALL BROS./EAST LIVERPOOL; impressed.
Globe Pottery East Liverpool	1881-1901	THE GLOBE POTTERY/ EAST LIVERPOOL, O. in a circle around a globe; stamped
Harker, Taylor and Company, East Liverpool	1846-1854	HARKER/TAYLOR & CO./ EAST LIVERPOOL, OHIO; impressed in a raised circle with a propeller like symbol in the middle of the circle.
Etruria Works East Liverpool	1855-1879	ETRURIA WORKS/1862/ EAST LIVERPOOL; impressed ETRURIA WORKS/GS HARKER & CO./EAST LIVERPOOL, O.; impressed
Richard Harrison and Company East Liverpool	1852-1853	RICHARD HARRISON/ EAST LIVERPOOL/OHIO; impressed in a circle
John Patterson and Sons Pottery Com- pany, Wellsville	1883-1900	J. PATTERSONS/WELLS- VILLE/OHIO; impressed

MANUFACTURER	DATES	MARK
A.E. Hull Pottery Co., Crooksville	1905-1917	H in diamond; impressed. H in circle; impressed
Salt & Mear East Liverpool	1842-1850	SALT & MEAR; impressed
John Goodwin East Liverpool	1844-1846	J. GOODWIN/1846; impressed
Weller Fultonham	1872-1948	WELLER; impressed.
Robinson, Ransbottom Pottery Co. Roseville	1910-present	R R P & CO/ROSEVILLE, OHIO/U.S.A.; impressed or stamped in black. (The black stamp is recent.)
D.E. McNicol Pottery Co., East Liverpool	1892-1954	D.E.MCNICOL/EAST LIVERPOOL, OH; impressed
U. Kendall & Sons Cincinnati	1845-1850	U. KENDALL & SONS; impressed
John Patterson and Sons Pottery Company, Wellsville	1883-1900	J PATTERSONS/WELLSVILLE/OHIO; impressed
Cassius & Josiah Thompson, East Liverpool	1868-1884	THE C. C. THOMPSON POTTERY CO./EAST LIVERPOOL, OHIO; impressed.
Brush Pottery Roseville	1925-1982	An ovoid container with four brushes having one letter of BRUSH between each brush and WARE on the container; blue stamp
Pennsylvania J.E. Jeffords & Co. Philadelphia	1868-1901	FIREPROOF/J.E. JEFFORDS & CO./PHILA./ PATENTED JUNE 28,
J.E. Jeffords & Co. Philadelphia		1870; impressed. DESIGN PATENTED NOV 13, 1879/L; impressed

MANUFACTURER	DATES	MARK
Jeffords (Cont.)		WARRANTED/JP/J/CO/ PEP/FIREPROOF; in blue diamond, stamped
John Bell Waynesboro	1833-1895	JOHN BELL; impressed JOHN BELL/WAYNESBORO; impressed JOHN W. BELL; impressed JOHN BELL/ WAYNES-BORO, PS.; impressed J. BELL; impressed.
Brockville Works Pottsville	1848-1852	BROCKVILLE WORKS/NEAR POTTSVILLE, SCH'L CO./PENNA; impressed.
J.B. Patterson Pottsville	?	J.B. PATTERSON/FIRE-CLAY WARE/MANUFAC-TORY/POTTSVILLE, PA; impressed.
Abraham Miller Spring Garden Pot-tery, Philadelphia	1840-1858	ABRAHAM MILLER; impressed ABM; impressed MILLER; impressed.
Pfaltzgraff Pot-tery Co., York	1811-present	PFALTZGRAFF POTTERY CO./YORK, PA; impressed (yellow ware produced from 1920 to 1930.)
Yellow Rock Philadelphia	?	YELLOW ROCK; in a circle, black or blue stamp.
Arthur, Burnham & Gilroy, Philadelphia	1854-1860	ROBERT ARTHUR'S/PA-TENT/2ND JANUARY 1855/ARTHUR, BURNHAM/ & GILROY/PHILADEPHIA; impressed in ellipse.
South Carolina Southern Porcelain Co., Kaolin	1856-1865	FIRE PROOF/SP CO; impressed S.P.C.; impressed.
Vermont Norton & Fenton Bennington	1844-1847	NORTON & FENTON/ BENNINGTON, VT.; impressed in a circle

MANUFACTURER	DATES	MARK
		NORTON & FENTON/EAST BENNINGTON, VT.; impressed.
Lyman, Fenton & Co Bennington	1847-1849	LYMAN, FENTON & CO./FENTON'S/ENAMEL/PATENTED./1849/BENNINGTON, VT.; impressed in a circle FENTON'S ENAMEL/1849/PATENTED; impressed in a circle FENTON'S PATENT/ENAMEL/1849/LYMAN, FENTON & CO.; impressed.
United States Pottery Co. Bennington	1849-1858	UNITED STATES/POTTERY CO./BENNINGTON VT.; impressed in ellipse with a cross above and below POTTERY CO.
A.A. Gilbert Bennington	1858-1859	A.A. GILBERT & CO; impressed
T.A. Hutchins & Co Bennington	1860	T.A. HUTCHINS & CO impressed.

Canada
CAPE ROUGE POTTERY
C.E.P. (Charles E. Pearson)
ST. JOHNS POTTERY
F.B. TILSON

England
SHARP's PATENT/WARRANTED/FIRE PROOF
T.G. GREEN/CHURCH GRESLEY CHURCH
GRESLEY/MADE IN ENGLAND
MADE IN ENGLAND
T.G. GREEN
T.G. GREEN & CO.

WOODVILLE/POTTERIES
WOODEN BOX
JOHN THOMPSON/WOODEN BOX/POTTERY/DERBYSHIRE
JOHN THOMPSON
G.S. READ/HARTSHORNE POTTER
WOODVILLE POTTERY
RAWDEN POTTERY
RICHARD STALEY & SONS/FIREPROOF

Part III:

IDENTIFICATION GUIDE

Pricing is not an exact science. Factors other than demand, scarcity, and condition enter into the formula. The region of the country, time of year, and a dealer's cost of doing business are but a few of the many influences. Unless a piece is marked, there should not be a considerable price variation. Depending on the rarity of the mark, prices can range anywhere from 20% to 100% above the price of an unmarked piece. Mocha decorated pieces run contrary to the rule of small price variations. The form of the piece and amount and intensity of the mocha can have a dramatic impact on the value of a piece. Thus, price variations can be significant.

Prices quoted are for pieces in perfect condition. Damage and missing parts will have a negative impact on price. The actual dollars and cents impact has to be judged piece by piece. In general, the more scarce the piece the less the price will be affected by damage. Flakes and hairlines will have less of an impact than chips and cracks. Lines in the glaze resulting from the age of the piece (crazing) are not considered damage, they are an indication of age. If the damage affects the decoration, it will have a greater negative impact on price than damage that does not touch the decoration. Despite these rules of thumb, it is ultimately the collector's decision as to the value of a damaged piece.

Unless a piece is marked or research has shown that it was produced by one pottery, no specific attribution is given.

It is impossible for every form and variation to appear in the Value Guide. If a collector encounters a piece that is not in the Value Guide, the best recourse is to estimate its value by comparison with similar pieces which are illustrated and priced. This is not a perfect solution but it is the only possible one.

Bowls

Produced by every pottery, bowls are the most common form of yellow ware. They were either thrown, molded, or pressed, and exhibited every type of decoration. Banding is the most common form of decoration. Pressed bowls which have a raised decoration covering either the entire bowl or parts of it came late in the 19th century. Mocha-decorated bowls are the most difficult to find. The sizes produced for home use range in diameter from 4" to 18". The smallest and largest sizes are the most difficult to obtain. The rims of bowls can be either rolled, extended, or both. A late 19th century development was a wide shoulder around the rim of a bowl.

Another form of bowl is the lipped or batter bowl. These were bowls with a pouring spout added. They can be found in diameters ranging from 7" to 15" with slip, mocha, or embossed decoration. The latter is the most easily found. Banded and mocha decorated batter bowls are very uncommon. Because of the various diameters, batter bowls as well as regular bowls can be collected in nests. The typical number of bowls in a nest is seven to nine.

A third form of bowl is the tea or waste bowl. The function of this bowl was to hold used tea leaves. It has a molded foot and flared sides. Given the function of the piece, it is much more delicate in appearance than a mixing bowl of similar size.

Plate 32a. A 6" diameter tea bowl with two wide white bands. Tea bowls are always rimless. They were made in the United States and England, 1850-1900. The form started in England during the 18th century.

Plate 32b. This 12" diameter batter bowl has a rare design of embossed leaves. It was produced in Ohio or England, mid to late 1800's. Note the foliated spout. While this is typically English, so many potters migrated to Ohio that it is possible that the bowl was produced there. Also, most batter bowls seen were made in Ohio.

Plate 32c. The light application of Rockingham glaze makes this mixing bowl an unusual piece. It dates from 1850 to 1880. These bowls are not easy to find and are usually not seen in smaller sizes.

Plate 32d. This 13" diameter mixing bowl is similar to ones sold by the Brush-McCoy Pottery in their "Dandy-Line." They called it the "Standard Yellow Ware of America" and marketed it during World War I. Zanesville, Ohio. These bowls were made in sizes 4½" to 14" in diameter.

Plate 33a. Made in New York or New Jersey, this is a unique decoration on this form. A rare piece of pottery! Mid to late 19th century.

Plate 33b. These American-made bowls, with their sparse decoration of blue or green seaweed, are fairly easy to find, especially in larger sizes. Most commonly found in larger sizes. Bowls with heavier and/or more well defined seaweed mocha decoration are not so easily found. Mid to late 19th century.

Plate 33c. This uncommon Ohio bowl has rust and white slip decoration over-sponged with Rockingham. Look for clarity of design when buying one of these bowls. Late 1800's.

Plate 33d. Found with many different combinations of slip decoration, these American mixing bowls are the most common form of yellow ware. They are very popular since they are the easiest and least expensive pieces of yellow ware to find. They were in production up to the mid 20th century.

Plate 34a. This Ohio batter bowl has an all-over drip glaze of Rockingham. These bowls are hard to find, especially in mint condition. If you look closely you will see an embossed pattern identical to that on plain yellow ware batter bowls produced by the D. E. McNicol company.

Plate 34b. Bowls with this amount of slip decoration are not commonly seen. Made in the 19th century, this one is attributed to the Jeffords Pottery in Philadelphia, because it has the diamond-shaped ink stamp on the bottom that was just one of three different Jeffords marks found on yellow ware.

Plate 34c. The white lining in this embossed batter bowl which is marked "J. E. Jeffords/Phila." puts an end to the belief that all white linings are British. The embossing on the Jeffords batter bowls is much fancier than batter bowls produced in Ohio and may have been influenced by early yellow ware from New Jersey.

Plate 35a. This banded batter bowl with a handle was made by the Weller Pottery in Ohio. Although a late development in yellow ware, they are very hard to find. They are not found in a wide variety of sizes – around 9" to 10" in diameter. 20th century.

Plate 35b. These 20th century American bowls are very desirable because of their size – only 4½" in diameter. They were the smallest yellow ware bowl made for utilitarian purposes and can be difficult to find.

Plate 35c. Possibly unique, this fancy slip-decorated tea bowl is 19th century, New York or New Jersey. Very few pieces with this type of decoration have ever been found. The decorator of this bowl used a slip cup with four openings to produce the flowing decoration.

Pitchers

Pitchers are one of the most interesting and desirable forms that exist in yellow ware. Ranging in size from 3½" to over 12", pitchers were either thrown or cast and had applied handles and spouts. Larger pitchers can have a lift lug applied to the front to aid in both carrying and pouring. Pitchers can be straight sided, ovoid, full and modified bulbous shaped, or pumpkin shaped. All types of decoration were applied to pitchers. As previously mentioned, the hound handled pitcher, especially those produced at Bennington, Vermont, represents the height of artistic development in yellow ware pitchers. Because this pitcher was produced by several British and American potteries, the quality varies. Damage is common to pitchers, especially on the spout and rim, due to the nature of their use.

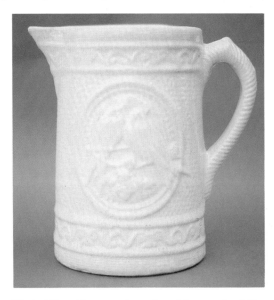

Plate 36a. Also produced in blue and white stoneware, this pitcher is a rare form in plain yellow ware. Midwest, circa 1900. The embossed design is named "Lovebirds."

Plate 36b. Because of both its form and decoration, this is a rare pitcher. Pitchers in this form are usually miniature – this one is 8" tall. The wide spout was formed from the body rather than applied. The mocha-decorated band is wider than normal and is enhanced by blue slip rings above and below it. 1860-1880.

Plate 36c. This 10" pitcher, dating from 1860-1890, holds over 1 gallon and requires a lift lug. Lift lugs, usually English, are found in form of a scroll, shell, and a lion's head.

Plate 36d. This pitcher can be attributed to the Jeffords Pottery of Philadelphia, since the embossing, applied handle, color & clay type are identical to that found on teapots signed by Jefford. Found near Philadelphia.

Plate 37a. Both of these pitchers are 7" tall. The one with the embossed collar was made in the Midwest. The one on the right is a Bennington form with a clear glaze. Plain yellow ware pitchers are very desirable. 1900-1930.

Plate 37b. This 6" tall pitcher with blue sponging can also be found in plain yellow ware. It is sometimes called a syrup pitcher. Midwestern; about 1920.

Plate 37c. These three banded pitchers were made in the Midwest. They can be found in other sizes than the ones pictured and show some of the variety produced in that time and place. First half of the 20th century.

Plate 37d. This pitcher is unusual because of its size, only 3½" tall, and the combination of black seaweed mocha and blue slip. The slip bands accent the seaweed mocha nicely. This pitcher has stoneware in the yellow ware body, giving it a slick "feel." Mocha-decorated pitchers of this size are not often found. England, 1860-1880.

Plate 38a. While many Rockingham-decorated pitchers can be found with embossed designs, very few are found in plain yellow ware. Hunt scenes such as this one were popular subject matter for design. This pitcher is 7½" tall; 1850-1890.

Plate 38b. The decoration on this pitcher is unique. It was probably made in New York or New Jersey in the mid to late 1800's. Very few pieces with this type of decoration have ever been found, so condition is not a big factor when purchasing one. 7½" tall.

Plate 38c. This short, fat pitcher could have been used to store batter. Its wide mouth makes it ideal for a mixing vessel, also. The lid (which is missing) extended over the spout to protect the contents. 1900-1930.

Plate 38d. With its heavy and well-defined brown floral seaweed, this is an example of a great mocha-decorated pitcher. Pitchers with this quality of decoration are not easy to find. 8½" tall and English or Scottish.

Plate 39d. This 10" tall pitcher shows a bi-colored seaweed design in brown and blue that covers nearly half the surface of the piece. The wide teal blue band near the bottom of the pitcher is unexpected and adds to the over-all design. England, 1860-1890.

Plate 39a. Well done clusters of cat's eye mocha make this a rare pitcher. Note how the skillful use of slip bands adds to the appeal of this piece. Very possibly made in southeastern Pennsylvania, 1850-1880. 8" tall.

Plate 39b. This set of three graduated pitchers with embossed cows and green highlights is hard to find. Single pitchers can be found but sets like this can be hard to assemble. Look for good detail in the embossing when buying. These pitchers can also be found in plain yellow ware and with colored overglazes. Midwestern, about 1900.

Plate 39c. A graduated set of three blue banded pitchers made in Ohio, first half of the 20th century. They were called "Zane Grey Jugs" by the Hull pottery co. They were made in six sizes – ¾pt., 1pt., 1½pt., 4pt., and 5pt.

Plate 40a. An unusually shaped pitcher with Rockingham applied in a design rather than an all-over sponge or drip pattern. A very hard-to-find piece of yellow ware. It may have been part of a bowl-and-pitcher set but there is no evidence to support this theory. Probably Ohio, late 1800's.

Plate 40b. This pitcher is another example of a piece of yellow ware that is very scarce (and much more valuable) when found in plain yellow ware. This pitcher, when covered with a Rockingham glaze, is quite common and valued at 20% of the plain yellow example. Midwestern, about 1900.

Plate 40c. This pitcher may be unique with its mocha design, known as oyster. An unusual clay mixture; very primitive. The blue slip bands add greatly to the over-all design. It is attributed to southeastern Pennsylvania, 1850-1880.

Plate 40d. With black floral seaweed over rust and white slip bands, this English pitcher is very unusual. Seaweed mocha is almost always applied over a white slip band, except in this case. 8½" tall. 1850-1880.

Plate 41a. A very rare, fancy slip-decorated pitcher in brown and white. The decorator of this piece has borrowed designs from the earlier pearlware mocha. Some of the thick slip decoration is missing; this does not affect the value as much as it would on a more common slip-decorated pitcher. This pitcher may be American and predate 1860.

Plate 41b. This pitcher is very unusual in plain yellow ware. The embossed design is called "Avenue of Trees." Note the crispness of the embossing and the orange highlighting. The green and black slip band is an interesting addition. 7" tall. Midwestern, 1900-1930.

Plate 41c. This design, called tobacco leaf mocha, is usually seen on cream ware and pearl ware made in England from 1790 to 1820. It is unique, so far. The form is also very different than most. Possibly American, 1840-1860.

Plate 41d. The embossing on this pitcher is known as basketweave and morning glory, and was made in blue & white stoneware, green glaze, and brown glaze. Look for clarity of design when buying. Midwestern, about 1900.

Plate 42a. The form of this pitcher and the placement of the banding and mocha decoration is unusual. On most pitchers the mocha band is centrally located. The form and clay color combined with the density of the blue seaweed make this an interesting and desirable piece. 1860-1880.

Plate 42b. This 7" tall pitcher has a floral and fern seaweed decoration covering half its surface. Mocha-decorated bands are not usually this wide. The amount and design of the seaweed are very striking. England, 1860-1880.

Plate 42c. This unusually shaped pitcher has two bands of slip-decorated with puffs of aqua blue seaweed The multiple dark brown slip bands make for more impact. It is probably American (Pennsylvania), 1850-1870.

Plate 42d. Of English manufacture, this 9" tall pitcher has a bicolored mocha design of brown and green. On the other side, the colors are reversed. Look for mocha-decorated pitchers with a well-defined "scene." 1870-1900.

Plate 43a. A rare pitcher with hundreds of slip dots similar to cat's eye mocha. Damage should not stop one from purchasing such a rare item. Firm attribution is impossible at this time but similar pieces have been found in Pennsylvania – too many to be coincidental. An early piece, dating around 1850.

Plate 43b. This hound-handled pitcher has an all-over brown glaze and is marked "AMERICAN POTTERY CO. JERSEY CITY" in a circle. Hound-handled pitchers of this quality are not easy to find. These were also made in Vermont and Ohio. Some damage is acceptable considering their rarity. They have also been found in plain yellow ware.

Plate 43c. This 8" pitcher, although somewhat plain, has an unusual combination of green and black seaweed mocha. These two colors are not often seen together. The design is unusual, too. England, 1860-1890.

Plate 43d. This alternate rib pitcher was made in Bennington, Vermont, from 1849 to 1858. It has a flint enamel glaze (green oxides on the Rockingham). Most of the yellow ware coming from this factory is highly stylized and glazed in a similar manner.

Plate 44a. Although these Ohio made pitchers are from the 20th century, they are hard to find. Small pieces of pottery are always desirable and these two pieces are only 4" tall each. The styles of the pitchers are very different, with one having a glossy glaze and embossed details, and the other being quite primitive.

Plate 44b. This 20th century Midwestern pitcher has a decoration of slip dots formed to look like flowers. Although a late item they are not easy to find. Covered crocks and custard cups can also be found with this decoration.

Plate 44c. A rare English pitcher with red and blue seaweed mocha in a decorative design. One of the ultimate pieces of yellow ware mocha, with its density of well-defined seaweed and a rare color combination. 1870-1890.

Plate 44d. An English pitcher with decorative banding and a rare blue seaweed mocha design of a basket and four flowers on each side. This pitcher is light in weight, without the slick feel when stoneware is added to the body. It exhibits great skill on the part of the maker. An early piece of yellow ware, 1840-1860.

Plate 45a. The artist who decorated this pitcher formed the earthworm into a spiral to make a flower-like design. This type of decoration is very rarely found, so damge is not a big consideration if you get the chance to purchase a piece decorated like this one. Note how the multiple white bands add to the design. Most likely made in England, 1830-1860.

Plate 45b. These three pitchers, decorated with earthworm mocha in combination with other types of decorations, are rare and possibly unique. England or southeastern Pennsylania, 1840-1880. A pitcher like any of the above has merit even if damaged.

Plate 45c. Rockingham pitchers like these were made with a variety of embossed designs and are hard to attribute unless marked. They are readily available in all sizes and shapes. Look for very good condition unless low cost and/or importance of design are factors.

Cups, Mugs, And Tankards

Manufacturers' price lists often made a distinction between cups and mugs. In their terminology, a mug is taller than a cup and any piece which is more than 4" tall should be termed a mug. However, the distinction is moot because mug is the standard term used by dealers and collectors to describe any piece under 5" tall. Straight sided, concave, or flared cylinders, mugs have either a plain or molded base and an applied handle. They were either thrown or cast and can be found with all types of decoration: plain, embossed, slip decorated, Rockingham glazed, and mocha-decorated. An interesting and desirable variation is the frog mug. A ceramic frog was attached to the inside bottom of a mug. The purpose was to frighten or repulse the drinker so that he would curtail his intake of liquid, usually whiskey or beer. Scarcer than cups and mugs, tankards are at least 5" tall and have a more slender appearance because they are taller than they are wide. The same type of decoration that was applied to cups and mugs was also used on tankards.

Plate 46a. This unusual mug has an embossed toby-like face and was made by the Bennett Pottery Co. of Baltimore, Maryland. The toby design is an English influence on American pottery. Pieces with this design were also made in New Jersey. Some toby mugs were not marked, so attribution can be difficult. These mugs are not easily found and are desirable because of the scarcity of the Bennett mark.

Plate 46b. Mugs are rarely found with lids. This mug and lid is enhanced by a strong application of blue seaweed mocha and dark brown slip rings. The decoration on the lid can vary slightly from that on the mug itself and still be the correct lid. Damage is less of an issue on a piece like this.

Plate 47a. Strong, tri-colored earthworm mocha decoration is the major factor in the valuation of this English mug. Although any yellow ware decorated with earthworm is rare and very desirable, this piece is exceptional because of the definition of the colors in the worm pattern and the way it was formed on the mug. 1840-1860.

Plate 47b. Shaving mugs are quite difficult to find. This one has a light application of Rockingham. These mugs can also be found in plain yellow ware and with green oxide over the Rockingham. They have been found in different sizes and shapes, too. 1860-1890.

Plate 47c. All the mugs in this photograph are fairly easy to find. A large collection of mugs and tankards could be very interesting considering the variety of sizes and types of decoration available. All of these mugs are American and date from 1890 to 1930.

Plate 48a. Rockingham-glazed tumblers are not commonly found. Expect chips on the rim of the tumbler. They were probably made in Ohio, 1880-1920.

Plate 48b. This yellow ware tankard has an unusual vertical sponge pattern in green. Tankards are not easy to find, but when seen usually have seaweed and/or slip decoration. 1840-1860.

Plate 48c. A tree and ground pattern in brown seaweed and an unusual combination of slip bands make this a rare tankard. Pieces like this mocha-decorated tankard are not often available, so some amount of damage would be acceptable. Most likely English, 1880-1900.

Plate 49a. Instead of the typical strap handle this Rockingham-decorated mug has an applied ring for just one finger. Probably Ohio, 1880-1920.

Plate 49b. A blue drip glaze and incised bands are the decoration on this unusual tankard which is impressed "PACIFIC" on the bottom. Another unusual tankard, and a piece which may be overlooked because it falls outside the traditional areas of yellow ware collecting. Always check the bottom of a piece of yellow ware for a mark. It may net you an interesting find.

49

Plate 50a. The exact use of these cups is a mystery. They are referred to as syllabub (or punch) cups. They are styled after English cups from 1810 and beyond and are not easily found. Circa 1870.

Plate 50b. These unusual handleless cups and saucers were probably made in England around 1900. They may have been made by Wedgwood, who produced dinner-service pieces in a hard, thin yellow ware. These cups and saucers are what is referred to as "demitasse" size because the cups are only 2" x 3" wide. A set such as this one would not be easy to assemble.

Plate 51a. This fairly common mug imparts some interesting information. Marked on the outside of the glaze is "McNICOL YELLOW WARE, EAST END PLANT TURNED BY J. C. CONNINGHAM 1919 OR 1920."

Plate 51b. Underside of mug in 51a.

Plate 51c. This mug has the rare decoration of red seaweed mocha. Red is the hardest color to find in seaweed. This mug is somewhat plain but because of its rarity should not be passed up. 1870-1900.

Plate 51d. This would be a great mug on its own, but it also has a large smiling frog on the inside. Frog mugs are rare and this one has the largest frog ever seen in a yellow ware mug. The frog is plain yellow, which is unusual in itself as most frogs have some degree of brown overglaze. A great piece!

Nappies And Milk Pans

Nappies and milk pans were standard kitchen items. Nappies, which were also known as deep sided baking dishes and cake pans, range in size from 4" to 15" and have flared sides with no lip. Milk pans, which were used to separate the cream from the milk are similar in form to nappies except that they have a rolled lip or rim and range in size from 8" to 15" in diameter. Of the two forms, milk pans are much harder to find. Pads in the form of hearts, triangles, rectangles, or flowers can be found on the bottom of some nappies.

Plate 52a. Look for good detail when paying extra for a nappy with flower or heart-shaped feet. They can be very worn due to the nature of their use. Heart or flower feet are generally not found on the smaller or larger nappies. Mid to late 1800's.

Plate 52b. Rockingham-glazed nappy with embossed flower feet. Unusual, embossed feet are harder to detect on these because of the dark glaze, so look carefully.

Plate 53a. Nest of plain and embossed nappies ranging from 8½" to 11" in diameter. Nappies were made by many potteries in the United States and England. They are fairly easy to find and are quite functional. Look for good condition when buying except in the case of a hard-to-find size and/or manufacturers mark. Some nappies can be attributed to a particular maker because of embossing. 1850-1920.

Plate 53b. Nest of milk pans with 8" to 15" diameters. Yellow ware milk pans are scarce, probably due to the fact that not many were made. Collectors are attracted to the rolled rim, which can vary in size. American, 1840-1870.

Colanders

Resting on a footed base with or without cutouts, a colander may best be described as a bowl-shaped form with holes for drainage. Two holes are also located near the rim so that a wire or string could passed through to hang the bowl. While generally scarce plain, banded and mocha-decorated colanders are rare. Colanders produced during the 20th century by both English and Ohio potters were embossed and often had a white interior. This is the most common form of colander. Although there is some controversy as to whether it was used as a colander or to bake pies, the pie plate colander is the rarest form. Resembling a pie plate with holes in the bottom, the form also has a flared lip and a foot rim. It can be found either plain or Rockingham-glazed.

Plate 54a. Two Rockingham-decorated pie plate colanders and a plain yellow ware one dated Oct. 8, 1861. These were made in the United States in the mid to late 1800's. Both kinds are hard to find but the plain yellow even more so. These are fragile so expect damage, especially between the holes.

Plate 54b. This 12" diameter colander has a very decorative application of brown and white slip. It was made in New York or New Jersey and may be unique. Since pieces like this rarely enter the market it is difficult to access their value because there is nothing to compare them to. 1860-1880.

Plate 55a. This rare colander was made in East Liverpool, Ohio around 1870 and is attributed to the D. E. McNicol Company. It has two sets of holes for hanging, which is unusual. While the form is great and the foot rim and hole pattern are decorative, it is the mocha decoration that makes it so rare. Worth buying in any condition.

Plate 55b. Shaped like a milk pan, this 11" diameter colander has large holes for quick draining. It was made in the United States in the mid to late 1880's and has a simple but pleasing form. These are not often found!

Plate 55c. Brown and white banded colanders are even more scarce than blue and white banded ones. This example is American, possibly made at the Yellow Rock or Jeffords potteries in Philadelphia, since similar examples (with blue and white bands) have been found marked. A great addition to a yellow ware collection! Expect damage due to the nature of use. 1850-1900.

55

Teapots And Coffeepots

Produced as early as the 1830s, both teapots and coffeepots were molded forms with applied handles and spouts. A coffee urn with a flint enamel glaze was also produced by Lyman, Fenton & Co. in Bennington, Vermont. This pottery also produced coffeepots and teapots with matching sugar bowls and cream pitchers. These matching sets were either Rockingham or flint enamel glazed.

Coffeepots can be found with Rockingham, sponge, plain, and flint enamel decoration. In addition to these types of decoration, teapots are also found slip banded and mocha-decorated. Of the two forms, teapots generally have the most intricate embossing. Due to their daily use, damage is common around the lid area and spout tip, and also on the base due to heat.

Plate 56a. This teapot has dripped blue glaze and embossing around the collar identical to flower feet on nappies. A bail handle was added to facilitate pouring. Teapots are very rarely found with this blue glaze and type of embossing. This one may have been made in Ohio or Pennsylvania, 1870-1900.

Plate 56b. This 1½ cup teapot has delicate embossing and is marked "AMERICAN POTTERY CO. JERSEY CITY." It is a typical example of the quality of early New Jersey yellow ware. While embossed teapots can be fairly easy to find, the opposite is true with an early, marked example such as this.

Plate 57a. This is an unusually large teapot and was probably made around 1840. If a teapot is interesting and inexpensive, it may be worth purchasing without a lid. 7" high.

Plate 57b. This teapot was made by the Jeffords pottery in Philadelphia and is marked with the patent date of November 13, 1879. These can be found in various sizes. The basket weave design shown on this teapot is very popular with yellow ware collectors. The clay is typically light and the glaze sometimes has a green or white cast to it.

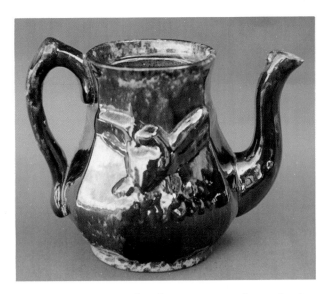

Plate 57c. An example of a teapot worth purchasing without the lid because it is embossed with and eagle and shield. Pottery with historical motifs is desirable to some collectors. The size and shape of this teapot is also interesting. 6" tall. 1870-1890.

Plate 58a. This tiny teapot embossed with grapes has the strainer at the spout tip instead of where the spout is attached to the body – an unusual characteristic. Probably made in England (possibly New Jersey); 1830-1860. 3½" tall.

Plate 58b. This teapot has an unusual color combination–well-defined green floral seaweed and blue slip bands. Mocha decorated teapots are rarely seen, so you can't be too choosy about condition. It was made in Ohio or England, 1850-1880.

Plate 58c. This rare teapot with blue floral seaweed may have been made in Ohio, 1850-1880. The seaweed on this piece is not as well defined as the green seaweed on the teapot above but there is no mistaking the "tulip" design on the mocha band. Another piece too scarce to bypass when it has damage.

Plate 59a. Although the molded pattern of "Rebekah at the Well" is the most common teapot found, the brown, red, and green glaze on this one sets it apart from the others. It is embossed "FIREPROOF SP. Co.", the mark of the Southern Porcelain (or Pottery) Co. It has unusually crisp detail. Only 5" high, it is rarely seen.

Plate 59b. This teapot held just one cup and is embossed with leaves and stars. It was made in England around 1840. An embossed design not commonly seen.

Plate 59c. This four-piece coffeepot is also referred to as a biggin. It is American and made around 1930. Its slick, grainy feel is indicative of stoneware in the body. The modern form is very different from the country image most people associate with yellow ware.

Pipkins

The function of a pipkin was to bake beans. The most common form is a rounded body with alternate ribs and a round, applied handle. This form was made in four sizes. The other form is similar in shape to a skillet and had a straight hollow handle to vent the steam. Both forms had lids and were either plain or Rockingham glazed.

Plate 60a. This pipkin has both a hole in the handle and a hole in the lid to vent steam. It is always found with a decorative Rockingham pattern on golden yellow ware. No firm attribution other than the fact that it is American. 1870-1900.

Plate 60b. This pipkin can be found with the mark of the Jeffords Pottery Co. or "YELLOW ROCK PHILA." It is a very popular form and increasingly harder to find. These pipkins are worth purchasing without lids albeit at a reduced price. One has also been found in this form but with a Rockingham glaze.

Plate 61a. Baking beans in a pot like this was popular in the early 20th century, which is when this Rockingham-decorated example was made. It would have had a matching pottery lid. It is midwestern in origin. Pipkins like this one were popular in other types of pottery as well. This particular pipkin is not often found. Many pipkins have lost their lids (as this one has) but still have merit. Price is for the one shown; a matching lid would raise the value 50%. This pipkin form is more commonly seen in blue and white spongeware.

Rolling Pins

An integral part of any collection, rolling pins are 9" long cylinders with removable, shaped, wooden handles. The handles are in two parts so that they can be slid into the holes at each end of the cylinder and screwed together. In addition to having advertising stenciled on them, rolling pins are either plain or banded. Plain rolling pins are uncommon. The other two types of decoration are very rare.

Plate 62a. The Brush-McCoy Pottery Company in Zanesville, Ohio, was one of the many potteries that manufactured plain rolling pins. At Brush-McCoy they marketed their pins as "Fancy Rolling Pins" and they were sold for $3.00-$4.00 per dozen. Since new wooden handles can be made, a rolling pin without the original handles should be considered, depending on the price.

Plate 62b. Banded rolling pins are very scarce and a welcomed addition to any collection. Since so few are available for purchase some damage would be acceptable. These banded rolling pins were probably also made in Ohio, 1880-1920.

Custard Cups And Pudding Dishes

Used to harden and serve custard and jelly, custard cups vary in size from 2½" to 4" in diameter. Cone shaped, custard cups have either a plain or rolled rim. They can be plain, slip decorated, Rockingham glazed, or sponge decorated. Pudding dishes, which are wider and more shallow than custard cups, were used to harden and serve pudding. The same type of decoration found on custard cups is also found on pudding dishes.

Plate 63a. Custard cups were made in many different shapes and sizes. The cups on the right and far right are easiest to find while the plain embossed and thin, cone-shaped cups are more scarce. 1880-1920.

Plate 63b. These Rockingham-decorated custard cups are particularly nice because they have a strong design. Since this type of custard cup is frequently seen, look for good color definition (like the ones pictured) and perfect condition. 1890-1930.

Plate 64a. Although these blue and white banded pudding dishes were made in this century, they can be hard to find, especially a set of four like these. The Rockingham-decorated pudding dish in this form is more commonly seen. Probably Ohio.

Plate 64b. These were called the Daisy Utility bowls by the Morton Pottery Co. They came in a set of six from 4" to 9" in diameter and had a green flower stamped on each panel. Although these shallow dishes resemble the pudding dish they were made for general kitchen use. It is possible to assemble a nested set like this one at a time.

Plate 65a. These two pudding dishes are the same form as plate 64b but without the decoration. The plain ones are usually only found in the 4" diameter size shown.

Plate 65b. These large custard cups with three white rings are not commonly found. This is the most difficult decoration to find on a custard cup. They may have been part of a line produced by the same company that produced the mugs, bowls, and rolling pins with the same decoration. Possibly Ohio, 1880-1930.

Plate 66a. This custard cup was made by the Weller Pottery in Ohio in the 20th century. Many of these custard cups are found impressed "WELLER" on the bottom. Matching pieces can be found in other forms.

Plate 66b. This is another form of the pudding dish but with a vining flower design stamped in blue. These dishes have stoneware in the body so are heavier and slick-feeling. They also have visible impurities in the clay. Look for good definition in the stamped blue design.

Plate 66c. Four pudding dishes with slip-dot flower decoration. This design is not often seen. It would take time to assemble a set like this one. Midwestern – 1900 to 1930.

Plate 66d. Custard cups with this color combination of bands are not easy to find. The blue and peachy-pink slip bands combine well on this primitive looking piece. 1880-1920.

Plate 66e. This banded custard cup is unusual with its cone shape. It resembles the pudding dishes in Plate 64a. These cups are not easy to find. This form is also found with a rust and white band combination.

Plate 66f. This type of custard cup was made by the Hull Pottery Co. in the early part of the 20th century as part of their Zane Grey line. They are fairly easy to find.

Pepper Pots And Master Salts

Usually 4" to 5½" in height, pepper pots are bulbous-bodied or skirted forms which rest on a pedestal base. A rim is almost always present beneath the pouring holes. Banded and mocha decorated pepper pots are more common than plain yellow ones. However, all are hard to find. Given their function, damage is to be expected, especially on the rim beneath the holes.

A master salt is a bowl 3" to 3½" in diameter which rests on a pedestal. The bowl can be either bulbous-shaped or straight-sided. The height of the entire piece is usually between 2¼" and 3". Master salts are either banded, mocha decorated, or plain; the latter are very scarce. Infrequently, one will encounter a master salt which rests on a footed base. The bowl is either banded or embossed.

Plate 67a. The master salt on the right is the form typically seen. The one on the left is much less common. They were most likely made in England between 1850 and 1900.

Plate 67b. This pepper pot has an unusual combination of green seaweed and blue slip bands. Heavy seaweed like this is not often seen on a pepper pot. The form is also a bit different. Probably England, mid to late 1800's.

67

Plate 68a. This green seaweed master salt with blue bands is an unusual and pleasing color combination. No specific attribution can be made as far as maker; the time frame is 1870-1900.

Plate 68b. This blue seaweed mocha-decorated pepper pot with chocolate bands has an unusual form. The dark bands give it definition. England, 1860-1900.

Plate 68c. These two mocha-decorated pepper pots were obviously made at the same pottery. The red seaweed trees and blue slip bands are great together. The black seaweed pepper pot with matching band is monochromatic but striking. Most yellow ware pepper pots have stone in the clay; these are pure yellow ware. Compare their clay color and texture to the other pepper pots in this chapter. 1850-1880.

Plate 68d. Banded pepper pots were made in many forms and combinations of slip decoration. They can be hard to find but are worth the effort. Some collectors like to match pepper pots with a similar master salt; it can be done. (Pepper pots did not come in pairs). The pepper shown is English, 1870-1900.

Plate 69a. Although these plain pepper pots were made in England relatively late in yellow ware production, they are rarely found. Because of this fact some damage would be acceptable. No other examples have been found, to date.

Plate 69b. This rare master salt has an embossed design of leaves and berries. It's rare for 3 reasons: it has embossing (as opposed to banding or mocha); it's plain yellow; it rests on a footed rim, as opposed to a pedestal base. This piece is, so far, unique. Circa 1875.

Plate 69c. This pepper pot has an unusual combination of black seaweed mocha on a rust slip band instead of the typical white band. The blue band on the rim makes for added interest. It is English, 1860-1880.

Plate 69d. This rare pepper pot was most likely made in England and is styled after ones made in luster decoration before 1850.

Mustard Pots

Cylindrical in shape with applied handles, mustard pots usually measure 2" high and 3" in diameter. They are either banded or mocha decorated and always have matching lids. On some mocha-decorated pieces, however, the lid may only have matching bands but no mocha. The lid will always have a wedge-shaped cutout for the spoon. Mustard pots can also be found with a pear-shaped body and a hinged, pewter lid. However, these are very rare.

Plate 70a. Even though the banding on the lid is a different color than on the base, this is the correct lid for this piece. Brown seaweed is not frequent in itself; this piece has a lot of it for its small size.

Plate 70b. As seen in this grouping, mustard pots vary in size and shape. The lids were easily broken, and some are missing, but they still have merit. Mustard pots are not commonly found. They date from 1850 to 1900.

Plate 70c. Mustard pot with incised lines, filled with blue slip. Expect damage on these pots around the rim of the base and on the edge of the lid. 1850-1900.

Plate 70d. This plain yellow, pear-shaped mustard pot originally had a pewter hinged lid. Only a few of these mustard pots have ever been found. Do not pass one up if the pewter top is missing – you may not get another chance. 1840-1880.

70

Storage Jars

Storage has always been of prime importance in the kitchen. While canning jars were used to store and preserve food for an extended period of time, storage jars were used to hold everyday kitchen staples and have them readily available for use. Humidors are a form of storage jars used to store tobacco. Found slip decorated, plain, Rockingham glazed, mocha decorated, and embossed, storage jars had either straight or canted sides. The decoration on the lids should match the base. However, because the lids were often made separately, there can be a slight variation in the color of the base and the lid. Most lids have a shaped finial to facilitate removing them. An exception is the lids on some small bowls which have a small circular indentation to help slide the lid off. Except for canister sets, which are discussed in another section, only hanging salt and butter crocks are found with their contents stenciled on the front.

Plate 71a. A rare form, these banded keelers are thought to have been used for cooling milk, but were probably made for general kitchen duty. They are very similar in form to drawings in Wedgwood's "shape book" (1770-1815) of "leg pans." Keelers can be found in many sizes and types of decoration. A few have matching pottery lids. Made in England and America, 1870-1910.

Plate 71b. This is called a Zane Gray Salt Box and was made by the Hull Pottery Co in Ohio in the early 20th century. They are still worth purchasing if the original wooden lid is missing – a new one can be made and does not significantly alter the value.

Plate 72a. This large cookie jar is a combination of yellow ware and stoneware, making it very durable. This one is more fancy than most other cookie jars. 1900-1940.

Plate 72b. These were made in England in the first quarter of this century and called rice jars. As you can see there was a style change somewhere along the line. They can be found in a few different sizes.

Plate 72c. This rare jar could have been used to store tobacco, however, its exact use is not known. The green seaweed has a blackish cast and the clay is very soft. It has a lot of decoration for a piece only 5" tall. 1840-1860

Plate 73a. These are two more variations of the hanging salt crock, both unusual in their decoration. The one on the left is different because the word "SALT" is stamped on in cobalt blue instead of the typical black. The salt box on the right has banding not normally seen on this form. Left, Ohio, 1910-1930. Right, Ohio or Pennsylvania, 1900-1930.

Plate 73b. This 5" high storage jar was probably used to store spices. It is too small and delicate to have been a preserve jar. 1890-1920.

Plate 73c. Still having its original lid, this rare mocha-decorated canister was made in Ohio, 1870-1890. The form of the jar and the style of the lid are different from most covered jars. Although the seaweed is not in a decorative pattern there is a lot of it, and the rust-colored slip bands are a nice contrast. 8½" tall.

Plate 74a. This covered tureen in the shape of a melon with an applied handle was made by the the C.C. Thompson Co. in East Liverpool, Ohio. Only a few of these have ever been found – they are extremely rare. A damaged example would be well worth purchasing since so few are around. 8" long.

Plate 74b. The exact use of this jar is a mystery. It is molded to look like a tree and has the face of Gladstone on the front. (Gladstone was a famous British statesman in the mid 1800's).

Plate 74c. This piece is marked "WEDGWOOD" and was obviously made to store honey. England, 1890-1920.

Plate 75a. These 20th century banded butter crocks come in a wide variety of sizes and decorations. They made were in many different potteries so attribution is difficult.

Plate 75b. Yellow ware sugar bowls are very hard to find. This one with its original lid and unusual blue seaweed mocha is a real find. England, 1850-1880.

Plate 75c. This unusual keeler has embossed horizontal bands and vertical "stripes" of brown glaze. Most keelers are found banded so this one is very special. 1850-1880.

75

Plate 76a. Rockingham-decorated sugar bowls were made by many different potteries in America during the 19th century. Attribution is difficult unless the piece is marked. Note the difference in the density and application of the Rockingham.

Plate 76b. A 20th century Midwestern butter crock with slip-dot flower decoration. Since these crocks can be hard to find one may be worth purchasing without a lid.

Plate 76c. This 8" tall Rockingham-decorated canister probably had a lid. This form is not often seen.

Plate 76d. This unusual Rockingham-decorated piece is from Ohio and was probably a batter jug or pail. It has a molded scene with people on each side. This form is seen frequently in decorated stone ware but not too often in yellow ware. It originally had a pottery lid and a tin cap to cover the spout. Circa 1900.

Plate 77b. This rare embossed sugar bowl was made between 1830 and 1860, possibly in New Jersey. Early pieces of yellow ware are so scarce that they are well worth purchasing damaged and/or incomplete.

Plate 77a. This rare sugar bowl is marked "ELSMORE & FOSTER CERES SHAPE TUNSTALL" with an English registry mark. Made during the 1860's, it is typically found in white ironstone.

Plate 77c. This 10" diameter crock has fancy handles and may have had a cover. It is English, 1870-1900.

Plate 77d. This 4" diameter blue seaweed mocha decorated crock could have been used to store food or tobacco. The amount and density of the seaweed mocha make it more valuable than a similar form with sparse decoration.

Plate 78a. A blue and white banded crock made in Ohio during the 20th century. It is missing its lid. Even though these crocks are later they are not frequently seen.

Plate 78b. Companies often advertised their stores or products on Midwestern pottery. Other than this beater jar you can find bowls, plates and rolling pins with similar advertising.

Plate 78c. This advertising beater jar still has the original egg beater and tin lid. Most jars are missing the beaters but a search of flea markets may produce one. 1910-1930.

Plate 78d. Since almost all keelers are found without lids this one is a rarity. Notice how the lid is cut out to fit around the tab handles. The handle on the lid is foliated. 1860-1890.

Canning And Preserve Jars

Found plain or with a Rockingham glaze, canning and preserve jars were critical to the storage and preservation of food. They were made in a variety of forms and different sizes with each form having several styles of necks and lips to accommodate the different types of seals: tin top, ceramic screw top, cloth, and wax sealer. Jars have been found with the marks of Edwin Bennett of Baltimore, Maryland, John Bell of Waynesboro, Pennsylvania, and "Robert Arthur's Patent/Philadelphia 1855." The introduction of the glass Mason jar and the superior durability of stoneware jars caused yellow ware jars to quickly fall from favor. All canning jars date from the mid to late 1800's.

Plate 79a. The jar at the far right is the most desirable of the group because it is marked with the Robert Arthur Patent, however all canning jars are sought-after. Attribution is difficult unless the piece is marked.

Plate 79b. This rare jar with an incised collar is marked "E. BENNETT'S PATENT." The Bennett stamp is faintly impressed just below the incised band. Do not pass up a jar like this just because it is missing its pottery lid.

Plate 80a. This unusual jar has delicate horizontal incising covering nearly its entire body. This decoration suggests it is of British manufacture.

Plate 80b. Jar marked "E. BENNETT'S PATENT, DEC. 8, 1856." This canning jar can also be found stamped on the shoulder. Another rarely seen piece.

Plate 80c. The jars in this photograph would have had either a tin lid or a wax sealer to secure the contents. Tallest jar is 7½" high.

Plate 80d. Very few preserve jars are seen with Rockingham decoration. These three jars have a good "mottled" look instead of the less desirable solid over-glaze. Note that all three also have a raised band at the center.

Plate 81a. Most jars with ceramic lids are found missing these lids. The presence of a lid can increase a jar's value by 50%.

Plate 81b. The Bell Pottery in Waynesboro, Pennsylvania, did not make many of these jars. They were impressed either "JOHN BELL" or "JOHN BELL, WAYNESBORO" on either the shoulders, the bottom, or both places.

Plate 81c. The octagonal jar is very desirable and hard to find. Rarely are they found with their original lids.

Plate 81d. This 6" tall canning jar is rare. The form and clay color are great!

Canister Sets

Although they are called condiment sets by some, canister sets would be more appropriate because these matched sets of containers were intended to store both food flavorings and food staples. The word condiment restricts their use to the storage of food flavorings. Believed to be manufactured only in the United States and during the 20th century, these sets consisted of various sizes of containers. The smallest size, about 5" tall, was for the storage of spices. The larger containers were for the storage of food staples such as cereal, coffee, and flour. As the popularity of these sets began to wane, manufacturers added additional forms to try to increase their popularity. For example, the Hull Pottery Company produced a set which contained a hanging salt, a butter crock, spice jars, a pitcher, custard cups, and a covered baking dish. The Brush-McCoy Pottery Co. in Zanesville, Ohio, produced a set which was called the "Dandy-Line" and advertised it as "The Lines That Sell In War-Time." It included 14 canisters, three sizes of custard cups, four sizes of butter pots, a pitcher, a rolling pin, seven sizes of nappies, seven sizes of bowls, and a sanitary pie plate.

Plate 82a. The small canisters (shown) were called spice jars and the large ones (plate 83a) cereal jars. Each came with six assorted names. Don't pass up these jars without lids as they are only devalued by one third by the loss.

Plate 82b. This set was also produced by the Hull Pottery Co. In addition to the pieces shown, a covered baking dish was available.

Plate 83a. These pieces were produced by the Brush-McCoy Pottery Co. and marketed as the "Dandy-Line."

Plate 83b. Brush-McCoy also produced a line of canisters decorated with bluebirds, but these are rarely seen. They were made in the spice (small) and cereal (large) canister size.

Molds

Molds are one of the most interesting forms in yellow ware and can be an entire collecting specialty. Oval, round, rectangular, and figural in shape, they can be found showing people, animals, foods, and flowers. Geometric designs are also found, and rarely ones with names or dates.

Another type of mold is the mini-mold which was used to harden either candy or chocolate. These are found mostly with geometric interiors. Many mini-molds are marked "YELLOW ROCK, PHILA."

The most common mold is an elongated octagon showing either corn, wheat, or grapes. These can be found with a white lining and marked "YELLOW ROCK, PHILA." Companies added the white interiors to their ceramics around 1900 because it was thought to make them more sanitary.

Most molds have some type of damage; due to the nature of their use it is to be expected.

Plate 84a. This rare mold in the shape of a turtle is quite large, measuring 6" by 8". It was made in the late 1800's.

Plate 84b. Three molds showing the variety of detail available in a rabbit mold. Each is 8" long and can be found in different sizes. The angular one is English, with a rough surface. The rabbit is the most common animal mold found. All date 1880-1920.

Plate 85a. This rare frog mold, only 5" long, has an unusual base that is oval and runs perpendicular to the length of the mold. 1850-1890.

Plate 85b. This large dark mold shows a somewhat indistinct pattern of a fruit cluster in the center. The design is small compared to the size of the mold, which is 8" long. Late 1800's.

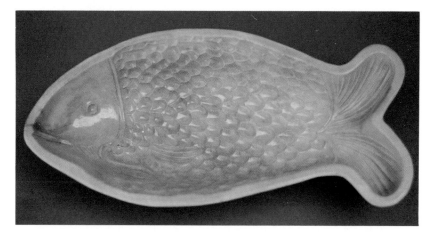

Plate 85c. This 12" long mold shaped like the body of a fish is rare because of its size and the fact that it is figural. Also, the fish is not often seen in a mold. 1850-1900.

Plate 86a. All of the molds shown in this photograph are unusual forms for a grape mold. The large, round mold is 9" in diameter. None of these molds is common. Eastern United States, 1870-1900.

Plate 86b. Two uncommon molds showing grapes. These two grape molds have great detail, an important consideration. 1840-1890.

Plate 86c. Fruit molds are hard to find, especially with good detail. The mold on the left is commonly found with shallow detail, so the one shown is better than most. 1870-1900.

Plate 87a. Swirl molds of this size, 4" to 5" in diameter, are fairly common. Molds like the ones in the photo can be found in sizes from 2½" to 7" in diameter. Look for the Yellow Rock stamp on the bottom – some are marked. Mid to late 1800's.

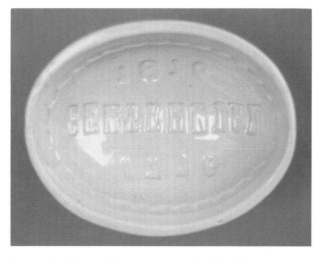

Plate 87b. This mold is impressed "CENTENNIAL 1776 1876" inside. It is very rare. This mold was probably made in England for the American market and is 5" long. It has also been found with a Rockingham glaze.

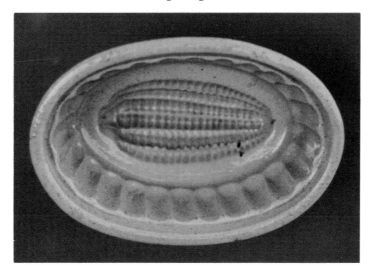

Plate 87c. Small oval corn molds like this one can be found marked by the Yellow Rock Pottery in Philadelphia. It is only 4" long and may have been used for an individual serving.

Plate 88a. Pineapple molds can be found in different styles and sizes. They can be hard to find. The pineapple has been used as a motif representing hospitality and is very popular. The mold on the right is similar to one made by Wedgwood in white ware c. 1810.

Plate 88b. This rectagular mold shows a cherubic figure surrounded by grapes. It is marked "I.W. CORY" from Trenton, New Jersey. Molds with figures of people are rarely found. Cory molds usually have an incised line around the outside perimeter of the rim.

Plate 88c. Animal molds, such as this 9" long mold of a lion, are very desirable. This mold is also desirable because of its fine detail. English, 1850-1890.

Plate 89a. This rare mold of a parrot on a branch has an unusual shape and is quite large – 8" by 10". Unlike most other molds this one has no fluting on the interior, giving it a plain appearance. Late 1800's.

Plate 89b. The mold in the center is the most common form of wheat mold; it can be found in graduated sizes. The other two wheat molds are not often seen. All three measure 6" to 7" long and date from 1870-1910.

Plate 89c. Most fish molds show a fish in profile; this mold shows the fish from a top view. You can feel a sense of motion with the water flowing by and the fish's wriggling body. Also adding value is the Rockingham-sponged exterior. Possibly Pennsylvania, 1850-1890.

Plate 90a. These molds were made in the three styles shown and in sizes from 5" to 12" in diameter. They are called turkshead (or turks cap) molds and are commonly found in redware. These examples are American, 1860-1900.

Plate 90b. This large mold of a bird sitting on a basket of fruit has good detail, an important factor when buying a mold. Detail may outweigh condition when buying a rare or unusual mold. Late 1800's.

Plate 90c. This rare mold of a flower was obviously made by the drape-molding process. The potter added 3 blobs of clay to the bottom to make primitive feet. 1840-1860.

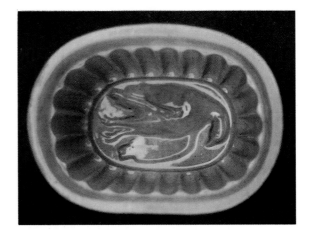

Plate 90d. This 5" long mold shows a rare design of a hanging game bird. This particular mold always has shallow detail. It was also made in white ware. England, 1850-1880.

Plate 91a. Just three of the many variations of style and size of the corn mold. These three molds measure 6" to 8" long and were made from 1850-1900.

Plate 91b. Both of these molds were made by I. W. Cory of Trenton, New Jersey. The smaller example shows Cory's impressed mark. The larger mold has shallow detail, which is negated by its rarity.

Plate 91c. This turkshead mold has a sponged pattern of Rockingham on the exterior only. This type of mold is much harder to find than a plain yellow example. Can be found in different sizes. American, 1850-1890.

Plate 91d. This mold is 5" long and shows a full-blown rose with buds and leaves. Yellow ware molds with flowers are rarely found. 1850-1880.

Plate 92a. This 8" diameter mold shows a design of a fig or pear with leaves and stars. Most molds that are round have only a geometric design. This one is very unusual. 1850-1900.

Plate 92b. This mini-mold is very desirable because of its heart shape. The Yellow Rock pottery also made another miniature heart-shaped mold without fluting. Both are hard to find.

Plate 92c. This 8" long melon mold is plain and is not often seen. It is patterned after similar molds made in white ware starting in 1800. 1850-1880.

Plate 92d. This rectangular mold has an unusual shape and design. It is believed to be a mold for blood pudding. Molds were used more for main dishes than for desserts. This mold resembles a loaf-pan. 1850-1880.

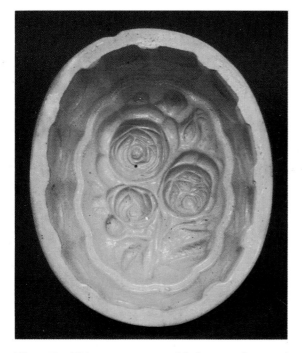

Plate 93a. This uncommon mold shows a cluster of roses and is 7" long. It is thick and heavy. When found, this mold typically has somewhat shallow molding. It may have been made by Cory of Trenton, N.J.

Plate 93b. This 5" long rectangular mold shows a well detailed fish and is hard to find. Fish have been a popular design for molds for the last two centuries. They can be found in almost any type of pottery or china. This bug-eyed fish mold has great detail. England, 1850-1880.

Plate 93c. This mold of a deer-like creature is unique, to date. It is most likely English since identical examples have been found in white ware. The fluting on the inside is more delicate than on other molds. 1850-1870.

Plate 93d. This Rockingham decorated mold has an embossed rather than impressed design, which is very different. Shown inside is "A. HANCOCK MANUFACTURER & INVENTOR" and a star in each corner. This is another loaf-pan type mold and can be found in plain yellow ware. 1860-1900.

Plate 94a. These four mini-molds marked "YELLOW ROCK, PHILA," are part of 15 known designs in the mini-mold form. The Yellow Rock company was the only maker of this size mold (usually 3" diameter). Not all examples are marked.

Plate 94b. This mold is only 4" long and has a primitive scallop shell design. The fluting on the sides is primitive, too. The exterior rim has a band of finely incised lines. This mold is very rare. It is English and dates no later than 1840.

Plates, Platters, And Baking Dishes

Pie plates are a common form of yellow ware. Ranging in diameter from 7" to 13", they were either molded, turned, or drape molded. The sides, which are usually 1" to 1¼" high, flare outward slightly from the base. Plates are found plain or with a flint enamel or Rockingham glaze. Marked examples, especially from the J.E. Jeffords & Co., can be found. Plates can be collected in nests of five to seven pieces. Although catalogs list square pie plates, an example has yet to be found.

Found only in plain yellow ware, dinner plates are approximately 10" in diameter and closely resemble a modern dinner plate. Price lists of some manufacturers also listed luncheon plates. However, none have been found. A square, scalloped-edged plate with scenes depicting the American West was produced for the American market by British potters during the early 20th century. Not only did the British potters produce plates in this design but they made entire place settings.

Serving pieces and baking dishes are not treated as separate forms since baking dishes often went directly from the oven to the table. Despite this duality of purpose, price lists often made a distinction. Serving pieces are either octagonal, oval, or rectangular in plain or Rockingham glaze. Oval serving pieces can be found with either scalloped or embossed rims. Three very scarce serving pieces produced by Lymon, Fenton, & Co. in Bennington, Vermont, were a relish dish, a covered butter dish with flint enamel glaze, and a covered serving dish with Rockingham glaze. Baking dishes or bakers come in either rectangular or oval shapes with slightly flared sides. Oval bakers range in size from 5" to 12" and can be marked. Likewise, rectangular bakers, which can be found in sizes from 5" to 14", can also be marked. Both forms may have white interiors. A few are found with heart-shaped feet. Although compiling them is a difficult undertaking, nests of both shapes can be assembled.

Platters are a scarce form in yellow ware. Bennett Brothers of East Liverpool, Ohio, as well as other potters produced an octagonal serving platter in plain yellow ware. Oval platters in plain yellow ware were also produced. Both forms can be found with Rockingham glaze, too.

Plate 95a. A nest of pie plates from 7¼" to 12" in diameter (like the one shown) is fairly easy to assemble. Pie plates that are 8" and under and over 10" will be the hardest to find. Marked examples and ones with shaped feet have a higher value. 1840-1890.

Plate 96a. These 7¾" round plates were probably some type of serving dish. They have a Rockingham glaze and an unusual molded design. 1870-1900.

Plate 96b. Rockingham baking dishes are quite easy to find and available in many shapes and sizes. Damage or repairs can be hard to see because of the decoration. Nested sets are possible. 1860-1910.

Plate 96c. While Rockingham pie plates are fairly easy to find, ones like this with heart-shaped feet are not. Since the Rockingham glaze tends to obliterate details you may have to look closely to see the shaped feet.

Plate 97a. This is an especially attractive baker with its deep rim and good color. It is 12" long and deeper than most other bakers. These dishes can be found quite a variety of sizes and shapes and are very functional. 1850-1900.

Plate 97b. Platters are rarely found and especially in plain yellow ware. Because of this fact condition is not paramount. 1850-1900.

Plate 97c. These pieces are called Westward Expansion or Westward Ho because of the embossed border of cowboys, Indians, and related elements. They are a thin, hard clay and are always a deep yellow. The plate is 11½" square. Other pieces in this set are cups and saucers, smaller plates, sugar bowls and cream pitchers.

Plate 97d. This piece is deeper than a platter but more shallow than a baking dish. It is marked AMERICAN POTTERY CO. JERSEY CITY, a hard-to-find mark. Pieces from this pottery are always a pale yellow. These platters can be found at least three other sizes.

Plate 98a. Dinner plates are rarely seen. This thick-walled plate has the name "Erna" under the glaze. It was probably made as a gift. 1850-1880.

Plate 98b. This dinner plate is marked ALLEN SOUTH AMBOY N.J. This a rare mark for a piece of yellow ware. Notice how this piece resembles a pie plate more closely than the dinner plate in plate 98a does.

Plate 98c. This 9" square Rockingham-decorated serving plate was made in Bennington, Vermont, from 1849 to 1858.

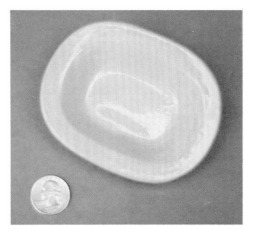

Plate 98d. This 4" long dish resembles a baker in form. They were known to have been made in England, where they are called patties. 1880-1920.

Plate 98e. Rockingham platters were made in East Liverpool, Ohio. They can also be found in an oval shape with embossing and both shapes can be collected in different sizes.

Flasks, Bottles, And Cow Creamers

Flasks and bottles come in a variety of forms of which most are figural. Although plain and slip decorated forms can be found, Rockingham and flint enamel glazed pieces are the most common. For example, book-shaped flasks, which were made in Bennington, Vermont, as well as at other potteries, were decorated with either a Rockingham or flint enamel glaze and came in 1 pint, 2 quart, and 1 gallon sizes. The 1 gallon size is the scarcest of the three.

Cow creamers were fanciful containers in which cream or milk was served at the table. Produced in both the United States and England, they are found with either a Rockingham or flint enamel glaze or in plain yellow ware. The latter are very scarce, while the Rockingham glazed cow creamers are the most common.

Plate 99a. This unusual piece is a cruet and still has its original pottery stopper. It is 10" tall and was made in Ohio, 1900-1930.

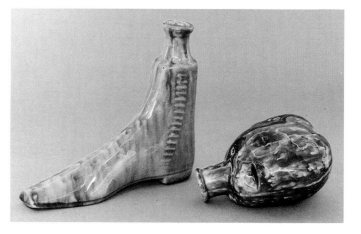

Plate 99b. A Rockingham-decorated shoe bottle, 5" high, and a potato flask which is 4½" long. These two fanciful flasks are hard to find. 1870-1900.

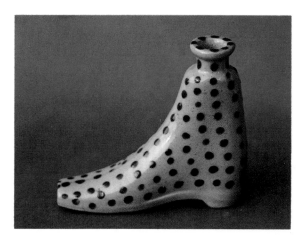

Plate 99d. This diminutive shoe flask or bottle has an unusual decoration of brown slip dots. Most shoe flasks have some type of brown sponging or over-glaze, so this flask is really unusual. It is probably English and made in the late 1800's.

Plate 99c. Under the embossed dogs the name "BULKLEY, FISKE & CO." is impressed. The company was a grocery vendor in New York City. Apparently they liked this method of advertising since other marked flasks have been found. However, these flasks are not common.

Plate 100a. Book flasks often had titles impressed on the spine such as BENNINGTON BATTLE, LIFE OF KOSSUTH, and HERMIT'S DELIGHT. These examples were made in Vermont and Ohio. Expect damage on the corners of the "book."

Plate 100b. Plain yellow ware cow creamers are so rare that it can be hard to assess them a value. One of the ultimate pieces for any yellow ware collection.

Plate 100c. Although Rockingham-decorated cow creamers from Bennington are more prevalent than their yellow cousins, they are not common. Expect damage to the horns, ears and/or missing lids.

Plate 100d. This rare rundlet is embossed "PALE COGNAC" on one end and "B.F. & CO." for Bulkley, Fiske & Co. on the other end. 1850-1880.

Plate 101a. This toby bottle, incised "JIM CROW," has great detail and an unusual application of Rockingham. Probably English, late 1800's.

Plate 101b. This rare English flask in the shape of a well-detailed fish is 10½" long. He looks as if he could come to life at any moment! These fish flasks can also be found in smaller sizes with a Rockingham glaze. 1850-1890.

Plate 101c. This Toby bottle is stamped "BILL" on the barrel the man is astride. Similar bottles were produced in Bennington, Vermont, between 1849 and 1858. This bottle is 8" high.

Plate 101d. The exact purpose of this 5" tall bottle is a mystery. Its plainness gives it a primitive look but it was made between 1900 and 1930.

Plate 101e. This is called a coachman or Toby bottle and was made in Bennington, Vermont from 1847 to 1858. They are found in different sizes and styles. This particular bottle is rare because it has certain details other bottles do not. Expect damage on the feet and hat rim.

Bedroom Pieces

Yellow ware was also found in the bedroom. Unfortunately, because of their intended use, many of the forms are not considered highly collectible. Neatly fitting into this category are bed pans, chamber pots, and foot warmers. Bed pans, which are found plain and with a Rockingham glaze, were available in a round form and in a shovel shape or French style. Chamber pots had applied handles and were available from retailers with and without lids. They were either plain, Rockingham glazed, flint enameled, slip banded, mocha decorated, or embossed. In plain yellow ware, foot warmers came in two shapes. The first was tunnel or loaf-shaped and had a knob on each end to aid in lifting. A round opening which was used to fill or empty the piece was on the top. The other was wedge-shaped or angular. This form also had a round hole on the top. Two shapes have been found with Rockingham glaze being the only decoration. The first can be described as broom-shaped with two concave troughs into which one's feet would fit. Probably a novelty item, the other form can be also be described as broom-shaped with the impressions of two feet. A very desirable addition to any collection is a pitcher and bowl set. As these two pieces have often become separated, it is worth purchasing individual ones. Often, the cost of assembling a set is less expensive but more time consuming that purchasing a complete set. Plain, slip-banded, Rockingham glazed, flint enameled, mocha-decorated, and sponge decorated sets can be found.

Plate 102a. Even though bedpans are not very desirable, it's a good idea to check the bottom for makers' marks. Pieces like these have been found with the Bennett/Baltimore mark. 1850-1900.

Plate 102b. Adult-size chamber pots were made in sizes from 7" to 10" in diameter. Both of these examples were made in Ohio, 1850-1920.

Plate 103a. Chamber pots with lids are not commonly seen. The addition of a lid can raise the value of a chamber pot 30-50%.

Plate 103b. Washbowl and pitcher sets are rarely found. This one has an unusual spout and an attractive Rockingham glaze. Most of the sets with this type of glaze were made at Bennington but no firm attribution can be made for this particular one. 1860-1890.

Plate 103c. This 19th century American-made foot warmer has an unusual wedge shape. Not easy to find, foot warmers usually have some form of damage because of hard use.

Soap Dishes

A very collectible form, soap dishes or drainers are found in a variety of shapes and sizes either plain, Rockingham-glazed, or flint enamel decorated. Regardless of whether the soap dish is round or rectangular in form, it has at least one hole in the top to carry off the water from the soap and one hole in the side to remove the water. Most soap dishes were made in one piece; others had a removable drainer and a lid to hide the soap from view.

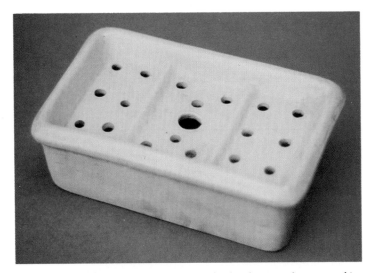

Plate 104a. This soap dish was meant for kitchen use because of its size – 6½" by 3½". Plain yellow ware soap dishes are hard to find and usually have some amount of damage due to the nature of their use. 1850-1900.

Plate 104b. Most soap dishes are hollow, like the piece shown left. However, a few are shaped like the one on the right. This open-form soap dish is even more rare in plain yellow than the hollow variety of the same color. A lot of the plain yellow soap dishes were made in Ohio, mid to late 1800's.

Plate 105a. This soap dish is unusual because it has only one hole for water drainage in the top. This design did not last long because it did not allow for enough drainage. This soap dish has a very pleasing form. 1850-1900.

Plate 105b. You could easily put together a collection of 25 of these Rockingham-decorated soap dishes exhibiting different form, color, and size. Since they are so prevalent their prices are still relatively low.

Plate 105c. This soap dish was made in Bennington, Vermont, in the 1850's. It had three pieces – base, drainer, and lid. The lid is missing. Most of these will be marked on the base with the circular 1849 mark.

Miniatures, Figurals, And Miscellaneous

Miniatures served no useful purpose. They were considered either a decorative or novelty item. Although some individuals have claimed that many of these pieces were salesmen's samples or items from children's play sets, there is no evidence to support either of these beliefs. Miniature chamber pots also known as potties or toy chambers are the most common miniature. They are either slip decorated, plain, Rockingham glazed or mocha decorated. Some have place names or the names of businesses stenciled on them. The scarcest miniature form is pitcher and bowl sets. They can be either slip decorated, Rockingham glazed, or mocha decorated. Other miniature forms include mugs, pitchers, crocks, jugs, cups and saucers, and various baking, cooking, and serving forms. Figurals were either decorative or decorative and functional. Examples of the latter type include inkwells, cow creamers, banks, matchboxes, Tobies, book flasks, and snuff jars. Purely decorative forms included cradles, animals, and shoes. These forms can be either plain, Rockingham glazed, flint enameled, mocha decorated, or sponged.

Also included in this section are forms which because of scarcity and/or limited variations in form and decoration do not need a separate category. A perfect example is a ladle. It is a very rare form, is always plain, and has no form variations.

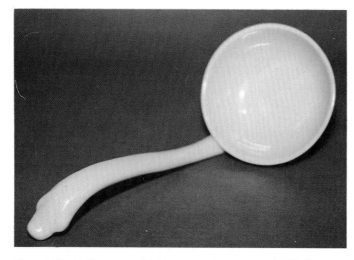

Plate 106a. Yellow ware ladles are rarely seen, probably because they were easily broken and possiby an experimental item. Do not let condition be a factor if you can purchase one. This ladle is 10" long.

Plate 106b. Yellow ware baskets are not common. Most are heavy and crude due to the amount of stone in the body. A late novelty item, 1900-1940.

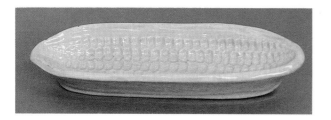

Plate 106c. This piece looks like a shallow mold but was actually used to hold an ear of corn at the table. Probably of Midwestern manufacture. Although they were made rather late, 1900-1930, they are not common.

Plate 106d. This is a curtain tieback. Most tiebacks seen were made at Bennington and have very little yellow showing through the glaze. This piece is a real find.

Plate 107a. Fancy pieces like these with gilt and sanded decoration are English or Continental and made during the Victorian era. Most are matchboxes; a few are toilet or pin boxes. They can be found in quite a variety of forms.

Plate 107b. The green and brown sponging on this pig bank is known as chicken wire. They were made in Ohio during the early part of the 20th century and are very popular with collectors. They can be found from 3" to 6" long.

Plate 107c. Yellow ware funnels are very rare, probably due to the fact that they were easily broken. Expect hairlines and chips if you are lucky enough to find one. They were produced in Ohio, 1850-1900.

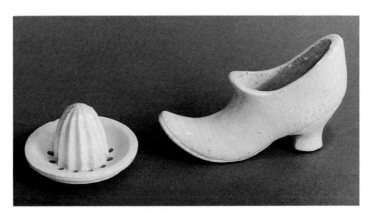

Plate 107d. These are two rare forms of yellow ware. The reamer was made for a practical purpose while the shoe is purely decorative. Both date 1900-1940.

Plate 108a. A Rockingham decorated funnel is even scarcer than a plain yellow example. Notice how the form differs from the funnel in plate 107c. The Rockingham decorated funnel has a wider mouth and a deeper rim to accomodate larger vessels.

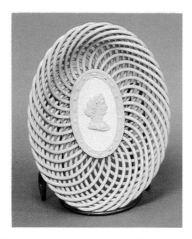

Plate 108b. Made in Victorian England, this piece was probably meant to be a candy dish. It features the bust of a woman and was formed from woven strips of clay. These "baskets" are found with gilt decoration as well as the white "sanded" decoration shown.

Plate 108c. This 4" tall iron is English and is fashioned after similar pieces made in the 18th century. It dates froom 1810-1840 and is not easily found.

Plate 108d. These were lids for large chamber pots. When decorated this well, they have enough merit to stand on their own. 1840-1870.

Plate 109a. This cradle was made in England 1810-1840 and is 4" long. Cradles like this one were popular novelty items in that time period and were made in different types of ceramics. Yellow ware cradles with Rockingham decoration have been found in three different forms. Expect damage on the rockers.

Plate 109b. Yellow ware banks are popular with collectors but unfortunately not many are found. They were made between 1890 and 1930. Other than the frog shown they can be found in the shape of fruit, barrels, and of course various pigs.

Plate 109c. Inkwells with faces are not common. The spaniel or a variation thereof is the most common form. Also, most inkwells have some amount of Rockigham decoration. These examples were made from 1860 to 1910.

Plate 109d. This flower pot and saucer were made 1900-1930 and have a yellow glaze over the clay, which is a mixture of stoneware and yellow ware. Flower pots have been advertised for sale since the mid 1800's but few have ever been found. Different sizes were made. The two pieces can be found separately.

Plate 110b. Even doorknobs were made from yellow ware! Most are covered with a solid brown glaze but this one has a transfer pattern applied to make it look like wood grain. Not often found. Mid to late 1800's.

Plate 110a. This piece is fashioned after an oyster barrel from Josiah Wedgwood's shape book. The raised rim was meant to be a pouring spout. They can be found with blue, white or brown bands.

Plate 110c. This hollow covered piece was made in Victorian England and fashioned after a doctor's bag. It was probably meant to be a candy dish. These pieces are also found in plain yellow ware.

Plate 110d. This candlestick was made in Bennington, Vermont from 1849 to 1858 and has a flint enamel glaze. Most of the sticks seen were made at Bennington. They can be found as small as 4¼" tall, but most are in the 7" to 10" range.

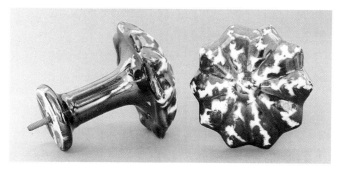

Plate 111b. These curtain tiebacks were made during the 1850's also in Bennington, Vermont. They are 4½" long and are rarely found.

Plate 111a. These Rockingham decorated candlesticks were made in Bennington, Vermont. Pairs are much harder to find than single sticks.

Plate 111c. These miniature jugs are 2½" to 3" tall and were probably made in Ohio 1880-1920. They are not common. The one on the far left is pure yellow ware clay while the others have stone in their clay and yellow in the glaze.

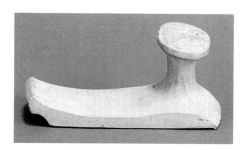

Plate 111d. This 5" long piece is made from yellow ware and was a tool used to shape yellow ware milk pans, bowls, etc. It was dug from the grounds around the pottery in Bennington, Vermont. Pieces like this one are usually found in museums and rarely come on the market place.

Plate 111e. Yellow ware washboards are rare, probably because few survived such hard use. Besides plain yellow, they are sponged in blue or brown glazes. Don't be fooled by stoneware or redware washboards with a yellow glaze. Expect chips or worn glaze. Ohio and Vermont are two known areas of production. 1860-1900.

Plate 112a. These planters are usually stoneware with a yellow glaze, but this one is true yellow ware. It was made circa 1930 and is 4" long.

Plate 112b. This form was also made in blue and white stoneware and was called a measuring cup. It was probably made in Ohio, 1890-1920. It is 6" high. The embossed design is called Spearpoint and Flower.

Plate 112c. This Midwestern pig bank has a slimmer body and darker yellow clay than the pig bank in plate 107b. It is 4" long.

Plate 113a. This 5" tall container was probably for some type of dry storage, but its exact purpose is not known. This form has been seen in blue & white spongeware but is unique in yellow ware, to date. 1890-1910.

Plate 113b. The body of this basket is a yellow ware/stoneware mixture. The applied handle is crudely done and the body was made in a mold. It shouts Art Deco with the molded design of a horse on one side and an unclothed lady on the other.

Plate 113c. This piece is similar in form to the measuring cup in this section, however, its exact purpose in not known. It looks as if it was made to go with Brush-McCoy's Dandy-Line. A rare piece at this time. 4" high.

Plate 114a. This basket is earlier and of finer quality than the other baskets in this section. It is 9" long. The molding is similar to a rice straw basket and the crude handle is in contrast to the rest of the basket. Great detail. 1860-1900.

Plate 114b. This mocha-decorated flower pot is very rare. It was made in Ohio circa 1900 and is 10" tall. Note the white lining. It is not known whether matching saucers were made.

Plate 114c. The exact purpose of these cups, which measure 2¼" to 3" tall, is not known, but they resemble some type of measure. They have a primitive appearance but may have been made into the early 20th century.

Plate 115a. This miniature jug has the original paper label from the Pearl China and Pottery Co. in East Liverpool, Ohio. It is probably from the 1930's.

Plate 115b. Rockingham decorated mini-jugs like this 3" tall example are found less often than their yellow counterparts. 1880-1920.

Plate 115c. Miniature chamber pots were a novelty item and were sometimes used for advertising purposes. They are an interesting choice of form for a novelty item. 1880-1910.

Plate 116a. Keelers can be found in many sizes. This example is only 3¼" in diameter. It has applied handles, unusual for a keeler. Possibly English, 1880-1920.

Plate 116b. These miniature pitcher and bowl sets, only 3" tall, are very rare. Sometimes the bowl and pitcher can be found separately, but the bowls are harder to find than the pitchers. The Rockingham example was made in Bennington, Vermont. 1880-1900.

Plate 116c. This is called a posset or porringer cup. This cup has a nice combination of blue, brown, and white slip decoration, which is unusual. Note that the rim of this piece slants up whereas the rims of the miniature chamber pots (plate 115c) are flat. The two forms are often confused because they are so similar. Posset cups are not easily found. This one is 3⅝" in diameter and has foliated handles. England, 1860-1880.

116

Plate 117a. Picture frames were only made in Bennington, Vermont. They were made in different styles and in sizes from 3" to 11" long. This frame is somewhat plain; other frames can be very ornate.

Plate 117b. This miniature covered casserole dish, only 2" in diameter, is a true salesman's sample piece. It is rarely found. It is impressed around the perimeter of the lid with the name of the company which marketed it. Pieces like this one are so small they can easily be overlooked. Midwestern 1880-1930.

Plate 117c. Spittoons and cuspidors were made by numerous potters. The spittoon, on the left, is common and mostly found with Rockingham decoration. When they are plain yellow they are rare. The cuspidor, on the right, is a form less often seen. Both pieces in the photo are unusual for their color and embossing. 1850-1910.

Plate 118a. These are two toy-size milk pans. They were not made for any utilitarian purpose. Small pieces of yellow ware of this quality are not often seen. 1850-1880.

Plate 118b. This funnel was made for use with liquids only due to its narrow tip. It was made in the Midwest, 1880-1920. There is stone in the body. It has a green sponge decoration with blue flecks.

Plate 118c. Egg cups can be found either plain, slip banded, or mocha-decorated, or with Rockingham. They are not often found. 1850-1900.

Plate 119a. These three miniature mugs each measure under 2" and have foliated handles. The slip decoration is in varying shades of blue. England, 1860-1900.

Plate 119b. This 4" tall banded piece has a form similar to an egg cup but appears to be too large for that purpose. The slip bands give it a strong appearance. 1880-1910.

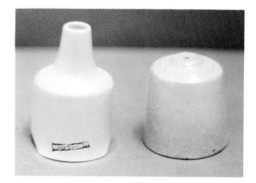

Plate 119c. Pie birds were placed in the center of a pie to vent the steam during baking. Both are of English origin. The one on the left is stamped "NUTBROWN." 1880-1920.

Plate 119d. This English wall plaque is 7½" x 11" and is very rare. It has an embossed design of a ram highlighted with a brown glaze and even an embossed "picture frame" border. There are two holes near the top for hanging. 1820-1840.

VALUE GUIDE

Bowls

Plate 32a 95.00-150.00
Plate 32b 150.00-195.00
Plate 32c..125.00-195.00
Plate 32d..125.00-175.00
Plate 33a ....1,700.00+
Plate 33b ....295.00-450.00 each
Plate 33c 125.00-225.00
Plate 33d ....65.00-95.00 each
Plate 34a 175.00-225.00
Plate 34b 175.00-275.00
Plate 34c 125.00-175.00
Plate 35a 100.00-150.00
Plate 35b 65.00-85.00
Plate 35c 450.00-550.00

Pitchers

Plate 36a 450.00-550.00
Plate 36b ....1,000.00+
Plate 36c..425.00-495.00
Plate 36d..325.00-375.00
Plate 37a
   Bennington..125.00-165.00
   Embossed collar 100.00-150.00
Plate 37b..90.00-150.00
Plate 37c
   Blue & pink banded..95.00-125.00
   Weller brown banded 95.00-110.00
   Gothic style 125.00-175.00
Plate 37d 450.00-550.00
Plate 38a 425.00-550.00
Plate 38b ....2,000.00+
Plate 38c, with lid..100.00-150.00
Plate 38d..975.00-1,150.00
Plate 39a ....1,150.00+
Plate 39b ....150.00-200.00 each
Plate 39c...95.00-145.00 each
Plate 39d..975.00-1,150.00 each
Plate 40a 325.00-425.00
Plate 40b 400.00-550.00
Plate 40c ....1,100.00+
Plate 40d..975.00-1,100.00
Plate 41a ....2,000.00+
Plate 41b 150.00-195.00
Plate 41c ....2,500.00+
Plate 41d 125.00-225.00
Plate 42a 495.00-695.00
Plate 42b 695.00-795.00
Plate 42c..595.00-795.00
Plate 42d..975.00-1,150.00
Plate 43a perfect ....1,500.00+
Plate 43b ....1,200.00+
Plate 43c..795.00-895.00
Plate 43d 550.00-650.00

Plate 44a ....100.00-150.00 each
Plate 44b 125.00-165.00
Plate 44c ....1,500.00+
Plate 44d ....1,250.00+
Plate 45a ....1,500.00+
Plate 45b ....1,500.00+ each
Plate 45c, depending on size ....75.00-225.00 each

Cups, Mugs, and Tankards
Plate 46a 395.00-495.00
Plate 46b 475.00-575.00
Plate 47a 850.00-950.00
Plate 47b 395.00-550.00
Plate 47c ....150.00-250.00 each
Plate 48a 125.00-175.00
Plate 48b 295.00-395.00
Plate 48c 450.00-550.00
Plate 49a 100.00-150.00
Plate 49b 275.00-350.00
Plate 50a ....125.00-165.00 each
Plate 50b ....125.00-150.00 each
Plate 51a& b 165.00-225.00
Plate 51c 350.00-450.00
Plate 51d 450.00-550.00

Nappies and Milk Pans
Plate 52a 150.00-225.00
Plate 52b 150.00-225.00
Plate 53a ....100.00-200.00 each
Plate 53b ....150.00-225.00 each

Colanders
Plate 54a
 Rockingham 395.00-425.00
 Plain 425.00-495.00
Plate 54b ....2,700.00+
Plate 55a ....2,500.00+
Plate 55b 500.00-600.00
Plate 55c 695.00-875.00

Teapots and Coffeepots
Plate 56a 450.00-550.00
Plate 56b 895.00-950.00
Plate 57a without lid 75.00-95.00
Plate 57b 425.00-500.00
Plate 57c without lid 75.00-95.00
Plate 58a 325.00-495.00
Plate 58b ....2,000.00+
Plate 58c ....1,800.00+
Plate 59a 395.00-495.00
Plate 59b 395.00-495.00
Plate 59c 150.00-225.00

Pipkins
Plate 60a 225.00-295.00
 without lid 100.00-125.00
Plate 60b 375.00-450.00
 without lid 100.00-150.00

Plate 61a without lid...125.00-150.00

Rolling Pins
Plate 62a 325.00-425.00
Plate 62b 500.00-600.00

Custard Cups and Pudding Dishes
Plate 63a ....20.00-35.00   each
Plate 63b ....15.00-22.00   each
Plate 64a ....65.00-85.00   each
Plate 64b, depending on size..65.00-125.00   each
   set of six..350.00-450.00
Plate 65a ....50.00-80.00   each
Plate 65b ....40.00-60.00   each
Plate 66a 20.00-30.00
Plate 66b 65.00-95.00
Plate 66c ....55.00-100.00   each
Plate 66d 30.00-45.00
Plate 66e 30.00-45.00
Plate 66f ....20.00-30.00   each

Pepper Pots and Master Salts
Plate 67a ....275.00-395.00   each
Plate 67b 495.00-595.00
Plate 68a 350.00-475.00
Plate 68b 400.00-500.00
Plate 68c
   Red seaweed...795.00-895.00
   Black seaweed 525.00-625.00
Plate 68d 325.00-495.00
Plate 69a 795.00-895.00
Plate 69b 350.00-450.00
Plate 69c 495.00-595.00
Plate 69d 400.00-500.00

Mustard Pots
Plate 70a 395.00-525.00
Plate 70b
   Blue seaweed 375.00-450.00
   Banded, blue and white 300.00-400.00
   Banded without lid...95.00-125.00
Plate 70c 300.00-400.00
Plate 70d 350.00-450.00

Storage Jars
Plate 71a ....300.00-400.00   each
Plate 71b 185.00-225.00
Plate 72a 125.00-150.00
Plate 72b ....150.00-175.00   each
Plate 72c 450.00-550.00
Plate 73a ....225.00-295.00   each
Plate 73b 150.00-185.00
Plate 73c 750.00-850.00
Plate 74a ....3,000.00+
Plate 74b 95.00-135.00
Plate 74c 125.00-150.00
Plate 75a, depending on decoration and size 150.00-225.00
Plate 75b 450.00-595.00

Plate 75c 250.00-350.00

Plate 76a
   without lid 125.00-150.00
   with lid 275.00-350.00

Plate 76b 125.00-175.00

Plate 76c without lid 120.00-160.00

Plate 76d complete 250.00-350.00

Plate 77a 395.00-450.00

Plate 77b without lid 150.00-195.00

Plate 77c 250.00-325.00

Plate 77d 395.00-495.00

Plate 78a without lid..75.00-125.00

Plate 78b 85.00-125.00

Plate 78c 100.00-145.00

Plate 78d 375.00-450.00

Canning and Preserve Jars

Plate 79a ....95.00-200.00 each

Plate 79b 195.00-250.00

Plate 80a 150.00-195.00

Plate 80b 195.00-250.00

Plate 80c ....150.00-225.00 each

Plate 80d ....125.00-175.00 each

Plate 81a ....110.00-195.00 each

Plate 81b 250.00-325.00

Plate 81c 175.00-250.00

Plate 81d 150.00-225.00

Canister Sets

Plate 82a with lid ....200.00-275.00 each

Plate 82b
   spice jars 135.00-185.00
   hanging salt with lid...150.00-225.00
   pitcher..100.00-150.00
   custards ....35.00-45.00 each
   covered baking dish (not shown) 95.00-125.00

Plate 83a
   bread canister 300.00-350.00
   sugar canister 225.00-275.00
   buttermilk pitcher...225.00-275.00
   hanging salt 225.00-295.00
   butter crock 150.00-185.00
   "cereal" canisters ....200.00-275.00 each

Plate 83b 250.00-295.00

Molds

Plate 84a 500.00-600.00

Plate 84b ....110.00-185.00 each

Plate 85a 500.00-600.00

Plate 85b 175.00-225.00

Plate 85c 450.00-550.00

Plate 86a
   left 145.00-175.00
   middle 175.00-225.00
   right..120.00-160.00

Plate 86b
   7" octagonal 150.00-185.00
   8" oval with blue sponged exterior 175.00-250.00
Plate 86c
   left 150.00-195.00
   middle 165.00-235.00
   right..125.00-165.00
Plate 87a ....75.00-125.00 each
Plate 87b ....550.00+
Plate 87c 85.00-110.00
   marked 125.00-150.00
Plate 88a ....175.00-275.00 each
Plate 88b 450.00-550.00
Plate 88c 450.00-550.00
Plate 89a 450.00-550.00
Plate 89b
   left 165.00-185.00
   middle 100.00-150.00
   right..165.00-225.00
Plate 89c 450.00-550.00
Plate 90a ....95.00-225.00 each
Plate 90b 475.00-550.00
Plate 90c 185.00-250.00
Plate 90d 295.00-350.00
Plate 91a ....110.00-165.00 each
Plate 91b
   large 185.00-225.00
   small..120.00-160.00
Plate 91c 110.00-165.00
Plate 91d 250.00-325.00
Plate 92a 295.00-350.00
Plate 92b 175.00-225.00
Plate 92c 175.00-225.00
Plate 92d 250.00-295.00
Plate 93a 250.00-325.00
Plate 93b 295.00-395.00
Plate 93c ....600.00+
Plate 93d ....495.00+
Plate 94a ....130.00-200.00 each
Plate 94b 395.00-495.00

Plates, Platters, and Baking Dishes
   Plate 95a ....100.00-175.00 each
   Plate 96a ....110.00-150.00 each
   Plate 96b, depending on size and shape................75.00-175.00
   Plate 96c 125.00-175.00
   Plate 97a, depending on size and shape..............125.00-300.00
   Plate 97b 400.00-525.00
   Plate 97c
      plate 175.00-250.00
      vegetable dish..275.00-325.00
      individual bowls ....125.00-150.00 each
   Plate 97d 400.00-550.00
   Plate 98a 225.00-275.00
   Plate 98b 225.00-275.00

Plate 98c...125.00-165.00
Plate 98d...125.00-150.00
Plate 98e...295.00-425.00

Flasks, Bottles, and Cow Creamers

Plate 99a 395.00-450.00
Plate 99b
  shoe flask...295.00-350.00
  potato flask 250.00-325.00
Plate 99c...495.00-600.00
Plate 99d...425.00-500.00
Plate 100a
  one pint..450.00-550.00
  two quarts 500.00-650.00
  one gallon..2,000.00-2,200.00
Plate 100b ....2,000.00+
Plate 100c...395.00-550.00
Plate 100d...450.00-550.00
Plate 101a 350.00-450.00
Plate 101b ....950.00+
Plate 101c...350.00-450.00
Plate 101d...95.00-125.00
Plate 101e...695.00-895.00

Bedroom Pieces

Plate 102a 25.00-65.00
Plate 102b
  slip decorated, without lid 85.00-110.00
  mocha decorated, without lid 125.00-150.00
Plate 103a 125.00-150.00
Plate 103b 1,150.00-1,350.00
Plate 103c...225.00-295.00

Soap Dishes

Plate 104a 295.00-375.00
Plate 104b
  left 325.00-375.00
  right...250.00-350.00
Plate 105a 325.00-395.00
Plate 105b 75.00-150.00
Plate 105c...325.00-375.00

Miniatures, Figurals, and Miscellaneous

Plate 106a ....750.00+
Plate 106b 295.00-395.00
Plate 106c...135.00-155.00
Plate 106d ....175.00+
Plate 107a ....95.00-325.00 each
Plate 107b 150.00-225.00
Plate 107c ....500.00+
Plate 107d
  reamer..200.00+
  shoe..200.00+
Plate 108a ....500.00+
Plate 108b 95.00-150.00
Plate 108c ....450.00+
Plate 108d ....175.00-225.00 each

Plate 109a ....395.00+
Plate 109b 150.00-200.00
Plate 109c ....150.00-250.00 each
Plate 109d 125.00-175.00
Plate 110a 150.00-200.00
Plate 110b 75.00-95.00
Plate 110c 250.00-295.00
Plate 110d 550.00-650.00
Plate 111a ....1,200.00+ per pair
Plate 111b ....450.00-550.00 per pair
Plate 111c ....95.00-165.00 each
Plate 111d ....175.00+
Plate 111e
 blue sponged ....650.00+
 plain ....695.00+
 Rockingham 425.00-595.00
Plate 112a 50.00-100.00
Plate 112b 195.00-275.00
Plate 112c 135.00-225.00
Plate 113a 195.00-250.00
Plate 113b 225.00-325.00
Plate 113c 225.00-295.00
Plate 114a 350.00-450.00
Plate 114b ....850.00+
Plate 114c ....75.00-85.00 each
Plate 115a ....125.00-185.00 each
Plate 115b 295.00-325.00
Plate 115c ....65.00-150.00 each
Plate 116a 250.00-350.00
Plate 116b
 mocha-decorated 1,350.00-1,550.00
 Rockingham-decorated 1,100.00-1,250.00
 banded 700.00-850.00
 individual pieces ....250.00-350.00 each
Plate 116c 225.00-325.00
Plate 117a 500.00-800.00
Plate 117b 225.00-295.00
Plate 117c ....75.00-175.00 each
Plate 118a ....150.00-185.00 each
Plate 118b 475.00-575.00
Plate 118c
 plain 195.00-225.00
 banded and Rockingham-decorated 375.00-475.00
 mocha-decorated 425.00-475.00
Plate 119a ....175.00-250.00 each
Plate 119b 225.00-295.00
Plate 119c ....100.00-150.00 each
Plate 119d ....950.00+

BIBLIOGRAPHY

Barber, Edwin A. *The Pottery and Porcelain of the United States: An Historical Overview from the Earliest Times to the Present Day*. New York: G.P. Putman's Sons, 1893.

Barrett, Richard Carter. *Bennington Pottery and Porcelain: A Guide To Identification*. New York: Crown Publishers, Inc., 1958.

————. *How To Identify Bennington Pottery*. Brattleboro, VT: The Stephen Greene Press, 1964.

Branin, M. Leylyn. *The Early Potters and Potteries of Maine*. Middletown, CT: Wesleyan University Press, 1978.

Clement, Arthur W. *Notes on American Ceramics: 1607-1943*. New York: Brooklyn Museum, 1944.

————. *Our Pioneer Potters*. York, PA: Maple Press Co., 1947.

Creswick, Alice M. *Red Book No. 6: The Collector's Guide To Old Fruit Jars*. Grand Rapids, MI: Alice M. Creswick, 1990.

Denker, Ellen and Bert Denker. *The Warner Collector's Guide To North American Pottery and Porcelain*. New York: Warner Books, Inc., 1982.

Gallo, John. *Nineteenth and Twentieth Century Yellow Ware*. New York: Heritage Press, 1985.

Gates, William C. Jr. and Dana E. Ormerod. *East Liverpool, Ohio, Pottery District Identification of Manufacturers and Marks. Historical Archaeology 16 (1-2)*. The Society for Historical Archaeology, 1982.

Hall, Doris and Burdell Hall. *Morton's Potteries: 99 Years*. Nixa, MO: A and J Printers, 1982.

James, Arthur E. *The Potters and Potteries of Chester County, Pennsylvania*. Chester, PA: Chester County Historical Society, 1945.

Ketchum, William C. *Early Potters and Potteries of New York State*. New York: Funk & Wagnalls, 1970.

————. *Pottery and Porcelain*. New York: Alfred A. Knopf, 1983.

————. *American Country Pottery: Yellowware and Spongeware*. New York: Alfred A. Knopf, 1987.

Lechler, Doris Anderson. *English Toy China*. Marietta, OH: Antique Publications, 1989.

Lehner, Lois. *Lehner's Encyclopedia of U.S. Marks on Pottery, Porcelain, and Clay*. Paducah KY: Collector Books, 1988.

Leibowitz, Joan. *Yellow Ware: The Transitional Ceramic*. Exton, PA: Schiffer Publishing, 1985.

McKendrick, Neil. *The Ninth Wedgwood International Seminar*. New York: Metropolitan Museum of Art, April 23-25, 1964.

McNerney, Kathryn. *Blue and White Stoneware: An Identification and Value Guide*. Paducah, KY: Collector Books, 1981.

Myers, Susan H. *Handycraft to Industry: Philadelphia Ceramics in the First Half of the Nineteenth Century*. Washington, D.C.: Smithsonian Institution Press, 1980.

Raycraft, Don and Carol Raycraft. *Wallace-Homestead Price Guide To American Country Antiques, Ninth Edition*. Radnor, PA: Wallace-Homestead Book Company, 1990.

————. *Collector's Guide To Country Stoneware And Pottery, Second Series*. Paducah, KY: Collector Books, 1990.

Roberts, Brenda. *The Collector's Encyclopedia of Hull Pottery*. Paducah, KY: Collector Books, 1980.

Spargo, John. *Early American Pottery and China*. New York: The Century Co., 1926. Reissued Charles E. Tuttle, Rutland, VT, 1974.

————. *The Potters and Potteries of Bennington*. Boston: Houghton Mifflin Co., 1926. Reissued Dover Publications, 1972.

Strong, Susan. *History of American Ceramics: An Annotated Bibliography*. New York: The Scarecrow Press Inc., 1983.

Schroeder's ANTIQUES Price Guide

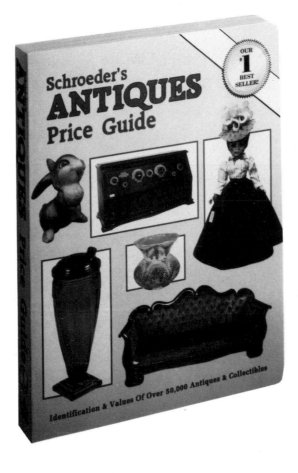

Schroeder's Antiques Price Guide is the #1 best-selling antiques & collectibles value guide on the market today, and here's why . . . More than 300 authors, well-known dealers, and top-notch collectors work together with our editors to bring you accurate information regarding pricing and identification. More than 45,000 items in almost 500 categories are listed along with hundreds of sharp original photos that illustrate not only the rare and unusual, but the common, popular collectibles as well. Each large close-up shot shows important details clearly. Every subject is represented with histories and background information, a feature not found in any of our competitors' publications. Our editors keep abreast of newly-developing trends, often adding several new categories a year as the need arises. If it merits the interest of today's collector, you'll find it in Schroeder's. And you can feel confident that the information we publish is up to date and accurate. Our advisors thoroughly check each category to spot inconsistencies, listings that may not be entirely reflective of market dealings, and lines too vague to be of merit. Only the best of the lot remains for publication. Without doubt, you'll find Schroeder's Antiques Price Guide the only one to buy for reliable information and values.

8½ x 11", 608 Pages   **$12.95**

COLLECTOR BOOKS
A Division of Schroeder Publishing Co., Inc.